# BIGGEST BOOK OF SHARKS & SEA CREATURES

**Text by**
Anton Ericson, Celia Brand, Donald Olson, Esther Reisberg,
Jane P. Resnick, John Grassy, Katharine Smith, Kerry Acker,
Mary Kay Carson, Rebecca L. Grambo, Robert Matero

**Photo Credits**
AdobeStock, Bigstock, Dreamstime, Fotolia, iStockphoto, Shutterstock

**Kidsbooks®**
PUBLISHING

**www.kidsbookspublishing.com**

Get ready to learn about
the amazing world of

# SHARKS and
# SEA CREATURES!

### Find out:
- How sea animals inspired stories
of mythical creatures
- Which groups of marine animals
can be seen from outer space
- Which ocean resident is the largest animal
that has ever lived
- Which sea animals have built-in sunglasses
- Fun facts about colorful fish, adorable
marine mammals, and scary sharks
- How you can help protect the ocean

And much, much more!

Also includes Search & Find® pages, mazes,
word searches, and other fun activities!

Get ready to impress your
family and friends with
your knowledge of
sharks and sea creatures!

**Kidsbooks®**
PUBLISHING

# Who Lives Here?

Try to imagine all the living things in the world—more than 10 million species of animals, plants, fungi, bacteria, and other types of creatures! Did you know that only 20% live on land? The remaining 80% are found in the sea.

## Up for Air

Sea mammals, such as whales and dolphins, cannot spend all of their time under the water's surface like fish. They must come up to breathe, just like people do. However, sea mammals can dive for long periods of time. The sperm whale can stay underwater for more than an hour, holding its breath while hunting giant squids.

## Staying Alive

As a lower link on the food chain, small fish have developed a great defense: swimming in schools. Because the fish swim together, darting left and right, predators have a hard time picking out a single fish to catch.

The octopus was once thought to be a monster.

The hermit crab scuttles across the sea floor.

Many sea creatures stay in one area of an ocean their whole life. Certain animals, such as the giant whale shark, below, roam the waters for food.

## Sink or Swim

Not all sea creatures spend their lives swishing their fins like fish or whales do. Many plants and animals live on the seafloor. Tiny plants and animals known as plankton simply float on the ocean currents.

The wide-mouthed manta ray can easily gobble up plankton.

## On the Chain

A food chain is made of links—living creatures eating other living things. It all starts with bacteria, which is partly dependent on the decomposition of dead animals. Bacteria provides nutrients to plankton and other sea life. Then the plankton is eaten by small animals that, in turn, are eaten by larger animals.

# Classifying Animals

Classification is the system scientists use to name and organize all organisms, or living things, into groups.

There are seven levels, or groups, of classification, and each group gets smaller and smaller from the first to the last. As you go down the line through each level, you'll notice that the smaller the group, the fewer animals it includes and the more those animals have in common.

The groups are called:

**kingdom**

**phylum**

**class**

**order**

**family**

**genus**

**species**

Sea star

Hermit crab

Nurse shark

A fun way to remember the order is to make up sentences using the first letter of each level. Here are a few examples:

**King Penguins Can Only Find Good Snacks**

**Keep Playing Cards Or Fun Games Somewhere**

**Kind People Classify Organisms For Good Scientists**

Green sea turtle

Regal blue tang

Sea creatures all belong to the animal kingdom, one of five kingdoms including plants, fungi, bacteria, and protists (single-celled creatures such as algae).

# What do humans have in common with the bottlenose dolphin?

## Let's take a look at how each species is classified to find out!

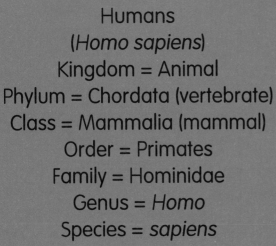

Humans
(*Homo sapiens*)
Kingdom = Animal
Phylum = Chordata (vertebrate)
Class = Mammalia (mammal)
Order = Primates
Family = Hominidae
Genus = *Homo*
Species = *sapiens*

Common bottlenose dolphin
(*Tursiops truncatus*)
Kingdom = Animal
Phylum = Chordata
Class = Mammalia
Order = Cetacea
Family = Delphinidae
Genus = *Tursiops*
Species = *truncatus*

# Our Oceans

Over 70% of Earth's surface is covered in water, and around 97% can be found in the oceans. When we talk about oceans, we often refer to one of the five named regions: Atlantic Ocean, Indian Ocean, Pacific Ocean, Southern Ocean, and Arctic Ocean.

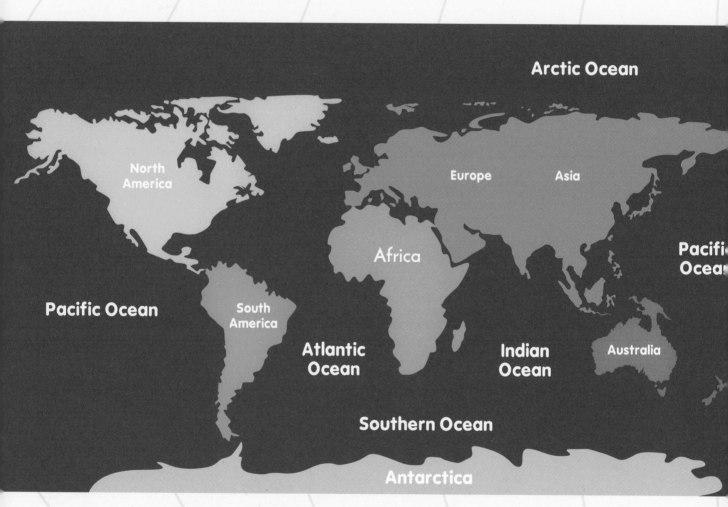

The three biggest oceans in the world are, in order:

the Pacific Ocean,
the Atlantic Ocean
the Indian Ocean.

Even though we refer to the five named areas as separate oceans, they are all connected to form one global ocean.

# Pacific Ocean

When Portuguese explorer Ferdinand Magellan reached an unfamiliar ocean on an expedition in November 1520, he and his crew found calm waters. He called the body of water *mar pacífico*, which means "peaceful sea" in Spanish and Portuguese. To this day, we know this sea as the Pacific Ocean.

The Pacific Ocean covers approximately 30% of Earth's surface! It is bordered by the Americas to the east of the Pacific Ocean basin, and the Australian and Asian continents to the west.

The Ring of Fire, a horseshoe-shaped stretch of volcanoes and earthquake sites, runs along the edges of the Pacific Ocean. There are a large number of active volcanoes along the Ring of Fire.

# Atlantic Ocean

The Atlantic Ocean is the beginning of what is known as the global ocean conveyor or global conveyor belt, a system of constantly moving currents that keeps ocean water circulating around the globe.

The Atlantic Ocean was named after the Greek god, Atlas, who according to Greek mythology was punished by Zeus and tasked with holding up the heavens.

# Indian Ocean

Lying between Africa and Australasia, the Indian Ocean boasts the warmest waters of all the oceans. It is over 23,000 feet deep at its deepest point in the Java Trench.

While they do not live in the sea or on the seaside year-round, Christmas Island red crabs migrate along the same path from the island's rain forest to the Indian Ocean's coast to breed each year. They take this journey during the rainy season, October to December, in order to keep their bodies moist.

# Arctic and Southern Oceans

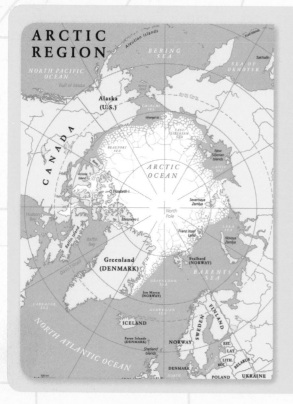

## Arctic Ocean

The Arctic Ocean is the smallest and shallowest ocean in the world, bordered by Russia, Canada, Greenland, Norway, and Alaska. The Arctic is partially covered in ice all year and is almost completely ice-covered when it freezes over in winter.

Impacts of climate change can be seen most obviously in the Arctic, where global warming melts the sea ice, threatening animal species such as polar bears.

Many endangered animals call the Arctic Ocean home, including the bowhead whale, one of the biggest whale species. Its huge head can take up almost one-third of its total body length, and its thick skull and large body help it to break through ice nearly 8 inches thick!

The North Pole, Earth's northernmost point, is located in the Arctic Circle. During the summer, the North Pole has 24 hours of daylight each day.

## Southern Ocean

The Southern Ocean is the newest named ocean, surrounding Antarctica and the South Pole. In 2000, the International Hydrographic Organization (IHO) established the Southern Ocean as the fifth major world ocean.

Southern elephant seals live in frigid Antarctic and sub-Antarctic waters, which are full of the fish, squids, and other marine animals these seals like to eat. This species is the largest of all seals. For about a month after birth, seal pups gain around 10 pounds a day! Southern elephant seals are called elephants for a reason—their trunks can be 1½ feet long!

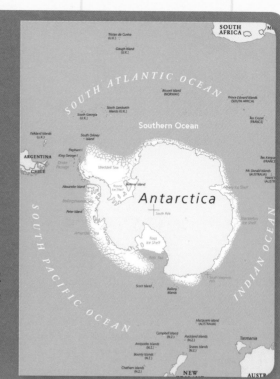

# Fill in the Blanks

## Secrets of the Sea

Fill in the missing letters to complete the fun ocean facts below. Then write the numbered letters in order at the bottom of the page to find out which sea creature is considered to be the largest animal that has ever lived!

The Pacific Ocean is the _ i _ g _ s t ocean in the world.
1

The A _ _a n _ i c Ocean got its name from a Greek god.
2

Surrounding Antarctica, the _ o _ t _ _ r n Ocean is the
3    4

most recent addition to the named global oceans.

This whale species breaks through ice with its
skull: bo _ _ e a _ .
5 6

Southern e _ _ p h _ n t s _ a _ pups gain about 10 pounds
7           8

a day for a few weeks after birth.

Volcanoes and earthquakes around the edge of the
Pacific Ocean make up the _ i n g o f F i r _ .
9

Answer: The _ _ _ _ _ _ _ _ _ !

# Food Chain

The relationships between organisms in the ocean, from the smallest plankton to the largest predator, can all be connected in a food chain divided into four levels: photo-autotrophs, herbivores, carnivores, and top predators.

## LEVEL FOUR — Apex Predators

Level four is made up of all the top predators of the ocean, like sharks, tuna, seabirds, and seals. They are apex predators, at the highest point of the food chain, that are fast, large, and good at catching prey. This level also includes humans, who hunt other top predators as well as those in level three.

## LEVEL THREE — Carnivores

Level three consists of carnivores, which include a diverse group of sea creatures that feed on various species from level two. Smaller carnivores like sardines and herring eat smaller zooplankton. Larger predators, like octopuses and many fish, eat larger level two herbivores, like crabs, lobsters, and small invertebrates, or animals with no spine or backbone.

## LEVEL TWO — Herbivores

Level two is made up of all the animals that eat the phytoplankton and other ocean plants. Small herbivores like zooplankton, jellyfish, barnacles, mollusks, and some fish in the larval stage drift around the ocean and eat any level one organisms they come across. Larger herbivores like surgeonfish, turtles, and manatees do the same.

## LEVEL ONE — Photo-autotrophs

Level one is the foundation of all ocean life. It is made up of photo-autotrophs, or single-celled organisms, called phytoplankton, as well as seagrass and seaweed. They absorb the sun's energy, nutrients, and carbon dioxide, and convert it through photosynthesis into organic compounds. In addition to playing a large role in the ocean, these plants provide half of all the oxygen humans breathe.

This is the most basic way to understand a very complex web of animal interactions. Humans have only identified 300,000 marine species and scientists think that there are millions more species yet to be found.

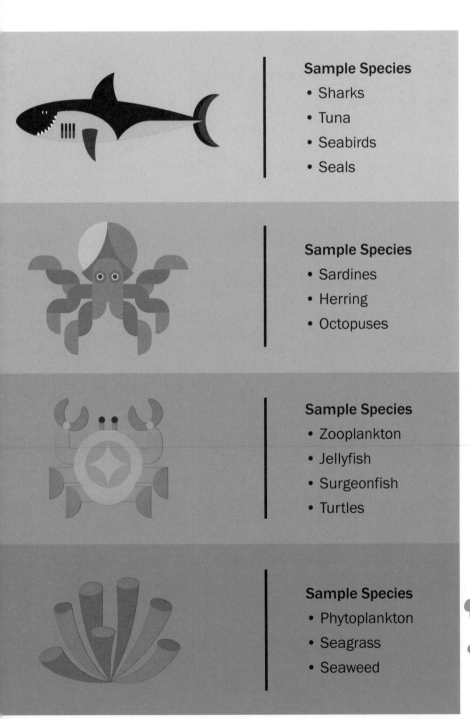

**Sample Species**
- Sharks
- Tuna
- Seabirds
- Seals

**Sample Species**
- Sardines
- Herring
- Octopuses

**Sample Species**
- Zooplankton
- Jellyfish
- Surgeonfish
- Turtles

**Sample Species**
- Phytoplankton
- Seagrass
- Seaweed

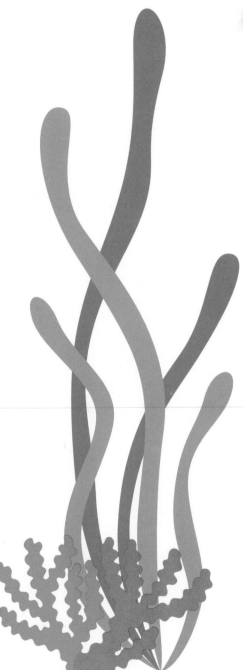

# PLANKTON

Plankton are microscopic organisms that live in the ocean. There are two kinds of plankton: phytoplankton and zooplankton. Phytoplankton are like plants: They make their own food from chemical production and live near the upper zone of the ocean to get sunlight. Phytoplankton are eaten by zooplankton, animal plankton that are, in turn, eaten by fish and other sea creatures.

As the first link in the food chain, plankton are vital to ocean survival!

Phytoplankton

Zooplankton

# Krill

Krill are tiny—only about 2 inches long—but they are extremely important in the ocean ecosystem! Krill eat phytoplankton and in return are eaten by hundreds of other animals, including fish, birds, and whales.

Antarctic krill are one of the largest of the 85 known species of krill. During certain times of the year, they gather in swarms so large and dense that they can be seen from outer space!

# emperor SHRIMP

The emperor shrimp develops symbiotic relationships, close relationships between two or more species, with nudibranchs and sea cucumbers. The shrimp will live on its host, which provides protection from predators, as well as an extra food source for the emperor shrimp. The shrimp walks up and down the host's body to find food that has been left behind or stirred up by the host. In return the shrimp will eat parasites off the host's skin.

## DID YOU KNOW?

A whale shark will eat 2.2 to 3.3 tons of plankton every day!

# Water Works

A fish is naturally equipped to live in water. It has gills for taking oxygen from the water, a swim bladder to keep it afloat, and other special adaptations.

**Pectoral fin**

## BREATHING

A fish breathes in by passing water through its mouth. The gill covers close to keep the water in. Then the gills remove the oxygen and pass it into the bloodstream. To breathe out, the mouth closes tightly and the gill covers open to let water out.

**Gill cover**

**Pelvic fin**

## ARMED WITH SCALES

A fish's overlapping scales are called armor because they protect the fish. Mucus, a slimy substance, moistens the scales, guards them from infection, and helps the fish slip through the water faster.

# Floating Free

Why don't fish sink when they stop swimming? Many have a swim bladder to help keep them afloat. The swim bladder is like a balloon inside the fish's body. By changing the amount of air in its swim bladder, a fish can stay perfectly balanced in the water without rising or sinking.

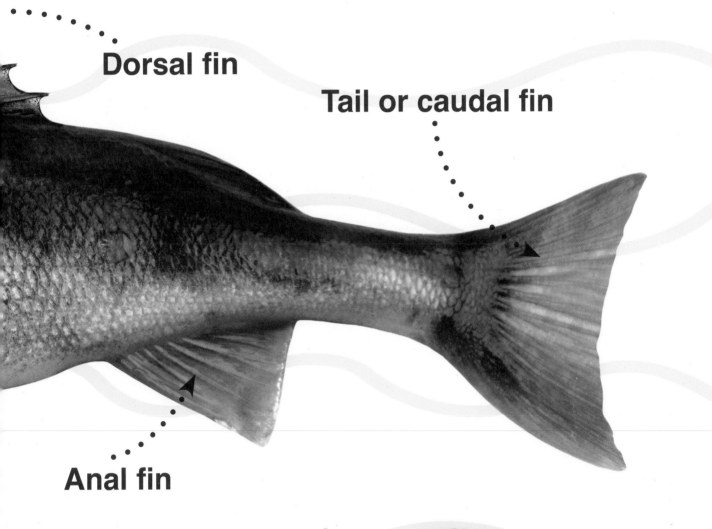

**Dorsal fin**

**Tail or caudal fin**

**Anal fin**

## Common Sense

Along the sides of a fish are the sense organs that help it swim around invisible objects in muddy water or keep perfect formations in a school.

# Porpoises vs. Dolphins

Porpoises, dolphins, and whales are members of a group of animals called cetaceans, mammals that have adapted to living in the water.

## TOTALLY TOOTHED

The majority of whales, including all dolphins and porpoises, have teeth. Instead of using their teeth to chew, most toothed whales only use their teeth to catch and hold prey before swallowing it whole. Orca teeth can be 4 inches long, perfect for grabbing seals right off the ice!

**AS THE DALL'S PORPOISE ZIPS THROUGH THE WATER JUST BELOW THE SURFACE AT HIGH SPEED, IT MAKES A FAN-SHAPED SPLASH CALLED A ROOSTER TAIL.**

## WATER PIGLETS

The porpoise probably gets its name, which means "pig-fish" in Latin, from being so short and chubby.

## ON THE HARBOR

These porpoises live in shallow coastal waters in the Northern Hemisphere, the half of the earth that is north of the equator, and they get their name from a tendency to swim in or near harbors. Harbor porpoises can dive over 650 feet, but they prefer to stay close to the surface.

# Echo Vision

Porpoises and dolphins are members of the scientific suborder Odontoceti, which includes all toothed whales. All odontocetes use echolocation, a process of locating objects by projecting sound waves and listening to the echoes, to find their prey.

# Smart!

PORPOISES AND DOLPHINS HAVE LARGE, COMPLEX BRAINS AND ARE EXTREMELY INTELLIGENT. THEY BOTH HAVE A STRUCTURE CALLED A MELON IN THEIR FOREHEADS, WHICH GENERATES SOUND WAVES.

**With so many similar characteristics, how do you tell dolphins and porpoises apart?**

There are certain physical features that distinguish the two types of animals: Dolphins have rounded, cone-shaped teeth and longer beaks, while porpoises have pointed, spade-shaped teeth and smaller mouths. A porpoise has a triangular dorsal fin, while a dolphin's dorsal fin is more curved or hooked.

# Great Adaptations

Penguins are an ancient bird family, found everywhere from Antarctica to Africa, New Zealand and Australia to South America and the Galápagos Islands. These tough, fascinating birds are specially adapted to life at sea—some penguins spend 75% of their time in the ocean!

**PENGUINS HAVE A SPECIAL GLAND THAT REMOVES SALT FROM WATER, SO THEY ARE ABLE TO DRINK DIRECTLY FROM THE OCEAN.**

## Color Coated

*Color counts when a penguin is trying to keep warm.*
*Black absorbs heat, and white reflects heat. A chilly penguin turns its black back to the sun and absorbs the warmth. A penguin in danger of overheating turns its white chest to the sun to reflect light.*

## Made to Molt

Most birds molt, or shed, old feathers and grow new ones. Penguins stay out of the icy water while they molt all at once—up to a month.

## Speed Slide

To move faster on ice, penguins toboggan. They lie belly-down on the ground, push with their feet and flippers, and glide like a person on a sled. This speeds them up from 2 or 3 miles per hour walking, to 8 miles per hour tobogganing.

No bird can dive like a penguin. A penguin will drop 70 feet just to grab a meal. Penguins are known to stay underwater for up to 18 minutes. Emperor Penguins have been observed 1,200 feet below the surface of the water—an amazing and probably rare dive.

## WATER WINGS

Ancestors of penguins could fly, but today's penguins only fly underwater. As penguins evolved to become better swimmers, they lost the ability to fly in the air because it took too much energy.

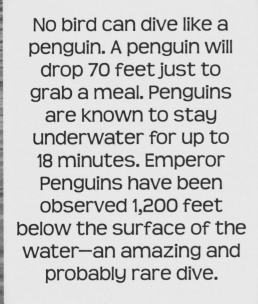

A thick-billed murre swims and flies.

## UP AND OVER

Going from water onto land is a simple task for penguins. When faced with steep walls of ice, snow, or rock, they leap, dive down, and then swim up so rapidly that they shoot out of the water—as high as 6 feet—and safely land on their feet.

## SHAPED TO SWIM

A penguin's body is shaped like a submarine or torpedo, sleek and streamlined, helping the penguin slice through water like a seal or dolphin. Their average swimming speed is 15 miles per hour.

## Leaping for Air

"Porpoising" is the penguin way of breathing while swimming. Penguins speed up underwater, shoot out above the surface, and breathe. Then they dive back under for another go-around.

# "Sea"-ing Stars

Sea stars, more commonly known as starfish, are part of a group of animals called invertebrates, which means they have no backbones or spines. Fish have backbones, so they belong to the group called vertebrates.

Scientists used to think sea stars could only sense light and dark with their eyes, but they now know sea stars can see. They won't be praised for their amazing vision any time soon, however: Sea stars can only see enough to recognize large, motionless structures, like their homes.

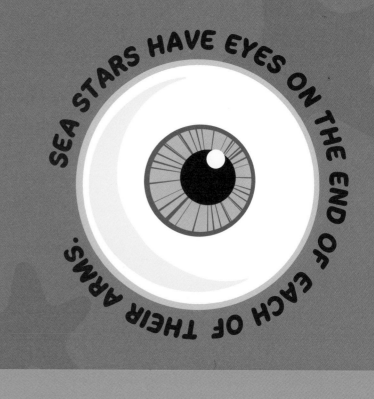

SEA STARS HAVE EYES ON THE END OF EACH OF THEIR ARMS.

A SEA STAR CAN WALK, FLIP OVER, AND STAND ON THE TIPS OF ITS ARMS, BUT IT'S NOT A FISH. FISH HAVE FINS, AND SWIM.

SEA STARS ARE CLOSELY RELATED TO SAND DOLLARS.

# Basket Star

The basket star is a type of brittle star, closely related to the sea star, that is found mainly in the deep sea. Its scientific name, *Gorgonocephalus eucnemis*, comes from the Greek language: *Gorgonocephalus* comes from the words *gorgós*, meaning "dreadful," and *cephalus*, meaning "head," and refers to the resemblance to the Gorgon from Greek mythology with its twisting serpents for hair! The word *eucnemis* comes from Greek words meaning "good leg."

**COMMON SEA STARS HAVE FIVE ARMS, BUT SOME SPECIES CAN GROW 10, 20, OR EVEN UP TO 40 ARMS!**

# SEA STARS don't have BRAINS.

# Fun Facts about
# Giant Clams

The giant clam can grow to be 4 feet long and weigh over 500 pounds. It is the largest bivalve, or animal with a two-part shell, in the world! Giant clams use their siphons, or tubes, to catch plankton for food and to absorb oxygen.

South Pacific legends describe giant clams as man-eaters, but this is far from the truth! The giant clam moves its shell much too slowly to catch a swimmer by surprise.

**GIANT CLAMS LIVE ON CORAL REEFS IN THE WARM, TROPICAL WATERS OF THE SOUTH PACIFIC AND INDIAN OCEANS.**

# Spot the Difference

## Hidden Jewels

Find and circle 10 differences between these two pictures.

Answers on page 299

# Lots of Limbs

Squids and octopuses live in an area of the ocean called the twilight zone, at a depth of 600 to 3,000 feet below the surface of the water.

## SUCTION CUPS

An octopus is all head, tentacles, and eyes. The underside of each of its eight tentacles is covered in suction cups. An octopus uses its sucker-covered tentacles to catch prey along the bottom of the sea. If an octopus loses an arm, it just grows a new one.

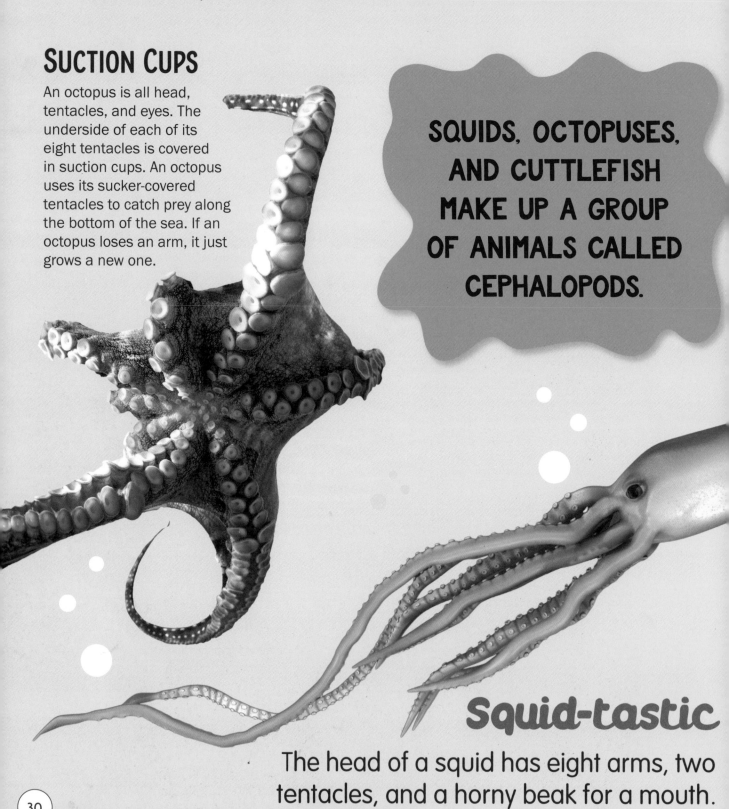

SQUIDS, OCTOPUSES, AND CUTTLEFISH MAKE UP A GROUP OF ANIMALS CALLED CEPHALOPODS.

## Squid-tastic

The head of a squid has eight arms, two tentacles, and a horny beak for a mouth.

An octopus can swim fast when it needs to: It jet-propels itself backward by shooting water out of its body. An octopus can also squirt an inky liquid at an enemy. The ink darkens the water, hiding the octopus and giving it time to swim to safety.

Squids have a muscly bag called a mantle that protects their vital organs and makes up most of their body length.

When an octopus spots prey, it will normally drop down on it from above and use its tentacles to pull the animal into its mouth. However, octopuses also crawl along the ocean floor, digging their arms into openings to search for food.

OCTOPUSES LIVE ALONE IN DENS THAT THEY HAVE BUILT FROM ROCKS. SOME EVEN HAVE DOORS THAT THE OCTOPUS CAN PULL CLOSED WHEN THEY ARE SAFELY INSIDE.

# Flipper Fun

Because sea lions and seals have flippers or fins, they are part of a group of sea mammals called pinnipeds, which means "wing-footed." Pinnipeds are semiaquatic, spending some of their time on land and some in the sea.

WALRUSES BELONG TO THE PINNIPED GROUP AS WELL.

## CALIFORNIA SEA LIONS

California sea lions can overheat when they lie on the sand, so they have to make sure they regulate their temperature. They cool off by resting a flipper in the water, fanning their flippers in the water, or flipping sand onto their backs.

## Seals and sea lions look pretty similar, so HOW CAN YOU TELL THEM APART?

### Sea Lions

- Sea lions have visible external, or outer, ear flaps.
- Sea lions use their front flippers to push themselves forward and their back flippers to steer when swimming.
- Sea lions move by rotating their back flippers and using all four flippers to support their body weight.
- Sea lions tend to be more social and vocal than seals.

### Seals

- Seals only have ear holes.
- Seals use their front flippers to steer, and their back flippers are used to power through the water.
- Seals move on land like caterpillars, shifting weight from the front to the backs of their bodies.
- Seals are not as vocal and social as sea lions.

The eyes of harp seals have lenses that help them focus on objects that are far away.

Harp seals' whiskers act like antennae. They can pick up vibrations in the water to help them find food to eat.

## DID YOU KNOW?

HARP SEALS HAVE NOSTRILS THAT CLOSE SO WATER DOESN'T GET IN!

Harp seals don't play musical instruments—they get their name from the harp-shaped spots on their fur.

# Fish in the Sea

All over the Earth, in streams, lakes, bays, and oceans, fish are swimming. There are at least 30,000 species of fish— more than any other kind of vertebrate. They come in a dizzying variety of shapes and sizes: Some are as long as a school bus, others could fit on your thumbnail. One thing they all have in common? They swim!

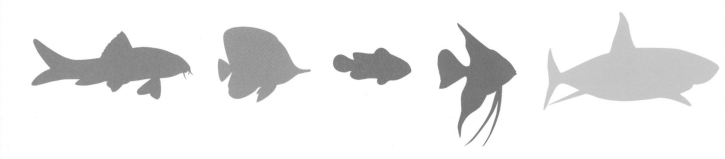

## Swimming in Style

To swim forward, fish sweep their bodies from side to side in a snakelike motion that goes from head to tail, with the tail giving the most kick. Some fish are faster than others. The sailfish, swimming about 60 miles per hour, is the speed demon of the sea.

# BONY-FINNED FISH

Most fish have skeletons made of bone. Bony fish can be divided into two groups:

Ray-finned fish have a fan of long, thin bones in their fins. Most fish you see are ray-finned fish.

Lobe-finned fish, like the Australian lungfish, have bones in their pectoral and pelvic fins that look a lot like the bones in your arms and legs. All the vertebrates that aren't fish—from salamanders to elephants—evolved from lobe-finned fish.

Ray-finned fish

# Functional Fins

Fins are important to a fish. The tail fin swings back and forth to push the fish forward. Dorsal and anal fins keep the fish from rolling over as it swims. Pectoral and pelvic fins are used for balance, steering, and braking.

# Penguins on Ice

Antarctica, covered by a sheet of ice nearly a mile thick, is one of the coldest places on Earth. This continent is the breeding ground of the Adélie, emperor, chinstrap, and Gentoo penguins. The emperor is the only penguin that spends the winter here.

The funny-haired macaroni penguin lives on the islands in the sub-Antarctic and Antarctic waters.

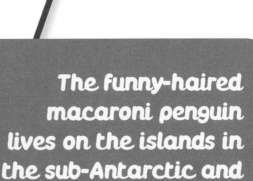

## Turns

a nest in
e it with
and
ng

## Jumping Gentoo

A white band that goes from eye to eye is the mark of the Gentoo penguin. This 14-pound bird, sometimes called the Johnny penguin, runs, jumps, and even slides on its belly on sand.

# PRECIOUS STONES

Stones are valuable to Adélies. Stones are the only material they have with which to build their nests in Antarctica. Sometimes the right-sized rocks are in short supply, so every Adélie watches its stones—or a neighbor will steal them!

## The Mating Game

In the mating season, all penguins head for land. Each species has its own territory, and some are very far from their ocean homes. The Adélies nest in the spring, which begins in October in Antarctica, but the land is still surrounded by sea ice. To reach their rookery, the penguins trudge across the ice—as far as 60 miles!

## LOUDMOUTH

The chinstrap is one of the brush-tailed penguins, which have long tails that sweep behind them. The chinstrap stands a little over 2 feet tall and has a black stripe across its chin. It also has an ear-splitting call.

## Chilly Winter

Emperor penguins start breeding in the winter, which begins in March. There is no sun at that time. The penguins stay on the grim ice for six months, until their chicks are ready to be on their own when summer arrives.

37

# Fish in Disguise

Some fish use disguises to hide from their enemies or catch their prey. Color and shape are the most important parts of a fish's camouflage: The right combination can make a fish look like a rock, a plant, or part of a bigger fish!

## It's a Blob!

The cuttlefish has many built-in defenses: It can change its skin color and texture to blend in with its surroundings, and it can squirt brown ink to cloud the water when danger is near. This amazingly complex creature also has a poisonous bite.

## Like a Rock

The scorpion fish is also called a rockfish or stonefish, because its skin flaps and feathery fins help it blend in with the rocks and coral along the ocean floor, safe from both predators and prey.

## Colors of the Rainbow

The octopus can turn many different colors. You can see the colors changing as you watch. The octopus has special, colored parts of its skin that it can make bigger or smaller within moments to hide itself on the seafloor.

## Two Shades to Hide

How can a big fish sneak up on its prey in the open ocean? Its coloring can help. Predatory fish like this tuna have dark backs and white bellies. When smaller fish look at the tuna from above, the tuna's back blends into the dark of the sea. From below, the tuna blends into the ocean's bright surface.

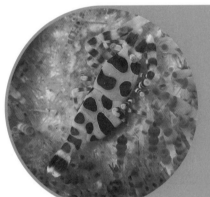

## On Fire

The coleman shrimp hides itself in the poisonous spines of the fire urchin so that it can escape predators.

Albacore tuna

## CAMOUFLAGE EYES

The crocodile fish's eyes help it blend in with the ocean floor and reefs where it hunts. The eyes have frilly iris lappets, fleshy flaps that make the pupils of the fish look more like the sand on the seafloor.

# Not a Doctor

Despite their name, surgeonfish do not perform medical operations! They are called surgeonfish because of the spines at the base of each side of their tails, which are sharp like surgeon's knives.

## Feeling Blue

Regal blue tangs and true blue tangs differ in appearance as well as habitat. While both are yellow as juveniles, the adult regal blue tangs of the Pacific are blue with a yellow tail and narrow black lines along their bodies. Blue tangs of the Caribbean grow to be various shades of blue with a lighter-colored spines. They are also known as Caribbean blue tangs and Atlantic blue tangs.

**Juvenile**

Regal blue tangs will often form schools of 10 to 12 individuals. They include different species of surgeonfish and tangs in their schools.

**Blue tang**

## Sea Surgeon

The razor-sharp barbs at the base of the surgeonfish's tail can be aimed so that a fish passing by can be slashed, sliced, or slit. As for people, the surgeonfish will gladly operate on anyone who grabs it by the tail.

**Regal blue tang**

# Word Search

## For the Birds

Look at the puzzle below and see if you can find the names of these seabirds. Circle the words going across, up and down, and diagonally. Some words may be backwards!

AUK
EIDER
FULMAR
GANNET
HUMBOLDT PENGUIN

KITTIWAKE
PETREL
PUFFIN
SEAGULL
TERN

| J | T | P | W | N | J | W | T | V | T | S | G | L | S | Q |
|---|---|---|---|---|---|---|---|---|---|---|---|---|---|---|
| I | W | V | L | Q | R | H | L | N | E | J | O | Z | P | D |
| K | G | O | L | Z | U | R | V | C | C | Z | N | G | F | H |
| B | N | F | U | Y | W | B | L | Q | Q | M | N | Y | M | A |
| N | I | U | G | N | E | P | T | D | L | O | B | M | U | H |
| T | U | L | A | F | Z | K | P | A | T | K | E | C | Q | S |
| B | E | M | E | T | O | D | A | E | P | U | F | F | I | N |
| K | U | A | S | P | X | V | N | W | Q | E | Y | N | D | H |
| K | F | R | B | R | Y | N | K | Q | I | Y | T | U | M | P |
| S | Y | X | Y | Z | A | J | I | U | Y | T | L | R | A | Q |
| N | M | S | E | G | E | D | E | L | A | W | T | P | E | H |
| X | L | J | T | I | I | W | A | H | R | G | U | I | H | L |
| V | U | U | D | Y | D | Y | Y | S | M | F | P | W | K | C |
| O | E | E | J | A | T | E | D | Q | I | H | I | O | J | Z |
| N | R | E | T | Z | Q | D | A | A | H | C | P | G | E | F |

# Crabby Critters

Crabs are crawly ocean creatures that belong to a group of animals called crustaceans. Crabs do not have a backbone, but a hard shell that protects them from predators.

## Coral Crab

Coral crabs depend on coral for shelter. Sometimes these crabs will have one claw bigger than the other. The larger claw is used for crushing and the smaller one is used for cutting.

## SKELETON CREW

Our skeletons are inside our bodies. A crab's skeleton is the shell on the outside of its soft body. The tough, flexible shell protects the crab. As the crab gets bigger, it outgrows, or sheds, its shell. Until its new, bigger shell hardens, the crab is not protected.

# Mating Call

Waving its oversized claw in the air, a male fiddler crab signals to females nearby.

**FOOD**

Hermit crabs live in second-hand seashells where they are protected from predators.

# BUG EYES

The eyes of a crab are beady and are on two stalks on top of their heads. The location of crabs' eyes helps them see more of what is around them, so they can spot their prey more easily. Crabs also have two antennae, which have smell detectors. These help crabs search for food.

# CRAB WALK

Since their legs bend sideways, crabs walk or crawl from side to side instead of forward and backward. They have 10 legs, two of which are sharp pincers, or claws. The crab uses these claws to dig for, hold, and carry food; crack open shells of prey; and warn attackers. Crabs eat meat and plants; they are both predators and scavengers.

# Helping Out

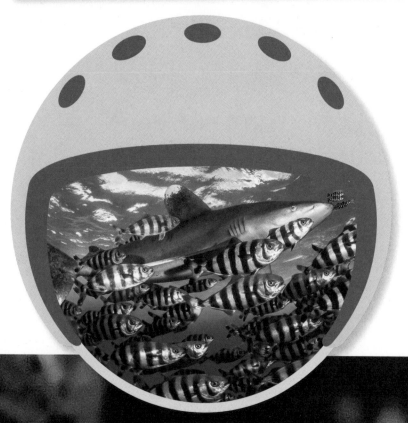

## PILOT FISH

Pilot fish have a type of symbiotic relationship called mutualism with sharks. A mutualistic relationship means that each animal benefits from the other. Pilot fish will stick close to the shark to hide from predators and eat the parasites that hurt the shark, and, in exchange, the shark doesn't eat the pilot fish. Pilot fish are often found in the mouths of sharks, swimming to eat the small pieces of food left behind from the sharks' meals.

## The Shrimp Cleaner

The Pacific cleaner shrimp is very social with other shrimp and with any larger fish that could be a potential source of food.

# Bon Appetit

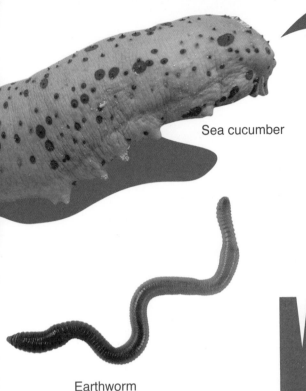

Sea cucumber

Did you ever wonder who keeps the ocean floor clean? Sea cucumbers help by eating the muddy surface and digesting what little food it contains.

Sea cucumbers are like the marine equivalent of earthworms on land: They break down algae, waste material, and tiny organisms and recycle them back into the ecosystem.

Earthworm

## KEEPING IT CLEAN

Fish can get parasites and infections and fungi. They get rid of them by visiting "cleaner fish" like the wrasse below. If bigger fish hold still, the wrasse will nibble away pests and dead skim. Even fierce predators let the wrasse work around their teeth without taking a bite. Cleaner wrasse often have a specific spot called a cleaning station where other fish can come to have the wrasse remove parasites and debris from their bodies.

Bluespotted ribbontail ray

Bluestreak cleaner wrasse

45

# Great White Sharks

Look out! It's a great white shark! These huge sharks, with mouths full of razor-sharp teeth, are the largest predatory fish in the sea.

Great white sharks **rarely** eat people. When they **bite** or **attack** a person, it's most likely because they have **mistaken** the person for a **sea lion.**

A great white shark's tooth can be up to 3 inches long.

| | | | | | |
|---|---|---|---|---|---|
| Inches | 0 | 1 | 2 | 3 | 4 | 5 |

Centimeters 0 1 2 3 4 5 6 7 8 9 10 11 12 13 14

Great white sharks have very **powerful** tails that can drive them through the water at *great speeds.*

These sharks have up to 300 sharp, triangle-shaped teeth arranged in several rows. You wouldn't want to be bitten by a great white shark!

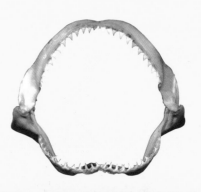

**DID YOU KNOW?**

SEA LIONS AND SEALS ARE SOME OF THE GREAT WHITE SHARK'S FAVORITE THINGS TO EAT.

7    8    9    10    11    12

16  17  18  19  20  21  22  23  24  25  26  27  28  29  30

# Pick Your Poison

## THE STONEFISH IS THE MOST POISONOUS FISH IN THE OCEAN.

The stonefish has 13 large spines on its back with very sensitive poison sacs attached to them.

THE BOX JELLYFISH HAS MILLIONS OF TINY, VENOMOUS HOOKS ON ITS TENTACLES.

The cone snail has a venomous tooth that it uses to paralyze its prey.

## Humans, Beware!

In a few species, the poison in only one puffer can kill up to 30 humans! In spite of that, the flesh is a delicacy in some Asian countries, notably Japan. Specially trained chefs carefully remove the poisonous parts, but the chefs know that one mistake could be fatal.

## Watch Your Step!

You don't want to step on a scorpion fish: Many have long spines, and some scorpion fish spines are poisonous. When a diver or swimmer steps on a spine, it shoots poison into the foot just like a needle. A scorpion fish's poison is strong enough to cause breathing problems and can kill a human.

A close relative of scorpion fish, the lionfish relies on camouflage and fast reflexes, rather than venom, to hunt.

Lionfish

# Into the Deep

Animals living in the deep ocean have adapted to the tremendous pressure of the water. Most are so perfectly adapted to this environment that they cannot survive for long when brought up to the surface—the change in pressure is just too much.

Deep-sea anglerfish have a glowing lure on their heads that attracts prey. When a fish comes near the anglerfish, it will get sucked inside the anglerfish's mouth and eaten.

# Weirdos of the Deep

In 1872, the Challenger expedition of British oceanographers proved beyond a doubt that there was life deep down in the ocean. Using scoops and dredges attached to ropes, they gathered samples of over 4,000 new marine organisms! Scientists have only recently begun to fathom the mysteries of the deep.

Gulper fish

## THE DARK SIDE

You don't have to worry about running into one of these fierce-looking fish. Fangtooths make their home in the very deep, dark part of the ocean. They can survive in frigid black waters as deep as 3 miles below the surface.

It is hard to find a meal in this Dark Zone, where there is no light, no plants, and few animals. Fangtooths eat shrimp, small fish, or anything else that happens by.

## VOLCANIC CREATURES

Deep down on the ocean floor are vents that spew out scalding hot water. Warmed by liquid rock inside the earth, these springs are rich in minerals. Giant clams, tube worms 12 feet long, and blind crabs and shrimp the size of small dogs, all live near hot-water vents. They eat a special bacteria that manufactures its own food from the vent's gases and heat.

The stomach of the viperfish can stretch to double its size.

The viperfish, and many other deep-sea fish, have see-through skin which helps them hide from prey by making them hard to spot when they are hunting.

Male anglerfish are very small and will attach themselves to the much larger female anglerfish as parasites.

# Penguins in America

Penguins only live below the equator. Some come ashore on Antarctica, frigid home of the South Pole, but others do not live in cold places. Magellanic and Humboldt penguins live on the coasts and islands of South America.

Humboldt penguins are found along the coasts of Peru and Chile in South America.

Baby penguins may be cute, but their nests certainly aren't. Humboldts and some other penguin species dig nests in guano, which is a fancy word for dried poop from seabirds!

It's hot!

## Can you imagine a penguin blushing?

This penguin can! The Humboldt penguin has patches of pink skin around its eyes and at the base of its bill, or beak. When it gets too hot, the penguin expels heat through the pink patches and through its feet and wings. It does this by sending blood to these featherless areas, so the rest of the body stays cooler.

# NAMESAKE

Magellanic penguins have a name from the history books. When Ferdinand Magellan, the Portuguese explorer, led the first expedition around the world in 1519, he sailed around the tip of South America. That's where the Magellanics live, on both the Pacific and Atlantic coasts.

I'm going for a swim!

HEE HAW

Magellanic penguins spend most of their time in the water, with the exception of mating and molting. Their torpedo-shaped bodies help them speed through the water at up to 20 to 30 miles per hour!

Like other penguin species, Magellanic penguins stick with the same mate to breed. HOW DO THESE PENGUINS PAIR OFF FOR MATING SEASON? Males will create a display and use vocalizations to attract females. Their calls sound like donkeys braying!

# Lobsters

There are many different kinds of lobsters, and they can be found in oceans around the world. Lobsters are crustaceans and are closely related to crabs. As lobsters grow, they molt, or lose their shells, so they can form new shells to fit their bodies.

**DID YOU KNOW?**

A LOBSTER HAS 10 LEGS!

Female lobsters can lay between 8,000 and 12,000 eggs. The eggs are tiny—only about the size of a single raspberry segment!

Lobsters use their stomachs, rather than their mouths, to "chew" or grind food.

Common lobsters, like this one, are not usually **RED** unless they are **COOKED**.

Lobsters have **poor eyesight,** so they get around using their **SENSE OF SMELL.** They **taste** with their **feet** and **listen** with their **legs.**

# Sea Snails

Snails are part of the mollusk family, meaning they have soft bodies, live in shells, and do not have backbones. Sea snails live in the ocean or salt water.

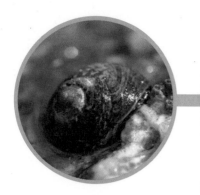

## Worldly Folks

Sea snails live all over the world, around coral reefs or attached to rocks and plants underwater. They can also be found under the sand on the ocean floor, looking for algae, dead plants, and other living things to eat.

## Around the Clock

Sea snail shells usually spiral clockwise, the same direction that hands move around a clock. Sea snails can make their shells bigger by adding calcium carbonate, which they get from the sea water, to the edges of the shells.

Most sea snails only eat PLANT material, making them HERBIVORES. However, there are some species of sea snails that eat other SNAILS and FISH.

# Maze

## Navigate the Nautilus

With its beautiful, creamy-colored shell and rust-colored stripes, the nautilus is highly sought after by shell collectors.

**Follow the maze from start to finish to get through the nautilus shell.**

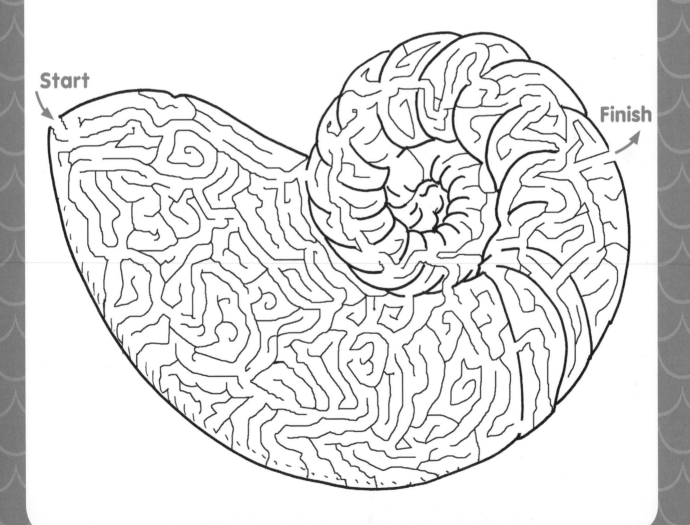

Start

Finish

# Fishy Ancestry

## Telltale Teeth

Fossil teeth are the best clues to shark evolution, telling us about sharks that existed millions of years ago—and where the oceans used to be. Scientists have found the teeth of the Megalodon, an ancestor of the great white shark, which lived about 12,000 years ago. It was huge, with 6-inch-long teeth—over twice the size of a great white's teeth!

## The Megatooth

The megatooth shark was a prehistoric predator that weighed as much as 110 tons—the same weight as 30 elephants!

Scientists think that the megatooth shark's bite was five times more powerful than that of a tyrannosaurus.

## The Drepanaspis

The Drepanaspis was a flat, paddle-shaped fish with a strange feature: Its mouth faced upwards instead of downwards. Scientists aren't sure how it ate, since it would have been very difficult for it to scoop up fish.

**The first animal with a backbone was the fish! They first appeared in the oceans over 500 million years ago.**

# THE DUNKLEOSTEUS

The Dunkleosteus, sometimes called the tyrannosaurus of the seas, was an armored fish with an extremely powerful bite. Instead of teeth, it had a beak made from pointed bony plates.

Scientists think that the Dunkleosteus was a cannibal, meaning that it ate other animals of its same kind, because they found bite marks on fossils from jaws that match the Dunkleosteus.

# THE LEEDSICHTHYS

The Leedsichthys may have been the largest bony fish to have ever lived. It was bigger than a killer whale.

The Leedsichthys was not a carnivore. Like modern-day basking sharks and baleen whales, this fish was a filter feeder.

# Sharks

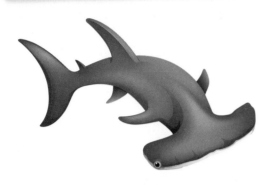

Terrifying, magnificent, mysterious: Sharks are masters of the sea. They're real survivors, built so well that they've had very little need to change or evolve in the last 150 million years. In some form or another, they've been around for about 400 million years. Even before dinosaurs roamed the land, sharks ruled the ocean.

## FAMILY MATTERS

Sharks belong to a group of fish called elasmobranchs (e-LAS-ma-branks). There are more than 780 species, and they are very different from one another. Surprisingly, most are fairly small. In fact, only 39 species are over 10 feet long. The largest is the whale shark, and the smallest is the 6-inch spined pygmy shark.

# Time Out

People used to believe that sharks never slept. That's not true. Scientists have observed more and more sharks taking time out to rest on the bottom of the ocean. Nurse sharks sleep in piles of up to 40 members.

## Senior Citizen

To guess how long sharks live, scientists now tag sharks in the wild and mark their vertebrae with a chemical. The shark's vertebrae have growth rings, which grow over time. Scientists can later count the rings since the marking and guess a shark's age.

## Meat Eaters

Almost all sharks are carnivores. They eat other fish—even other sharks—and sea mammals like dolphins and seals. Some feed at the surface on plankton. Bottom-dwelling sharks feed on crustaceans, such as crabs, and mollusks, such as clams, crunching them with specialized teeth.

# Ancient Fish-story

## DO NOT DISTURB

In 1938, fishermen in the Western Indian Ocean netted a coelacanth, a fish believed to have been extinct for 65 million years! Scientists speculated that it had been living undisturbed in the deep sea. Coelacanths are known as living fossils.

The ancient Greeks dubbed sea sponges *zoofitan*, meaning "half-plant, half-animal." Scientists eventually reclassified sea sponges as animals, although they survive, reproduce, and act more like plants do.

Sea sponges come in all different shapes and sizes. They can look like tubes, webs, or even golf balls! A sea sponge the size of a minivan was discovered during a deep-sea expedition in 2015.

# THE COELACANTH

The coelacanth (SEEL-uh-kanth) got its genus name, *Latimeria*, from its discoverer, museum curator Marjorie Courtenay-Latimer. There are two known species of coelacanths: the *Latimeria chalumnae*, found in the Western Indian Ocean off the coast of the Comoros Islands, and the *Latimeria menadoensis*, discovered in 1997 in the waters near Sulawesi, Indonesia.

## DID YOU KNOW?

Scientists believe the sea sponge was the earliest living multicellular creature on earth. It was alive 640 million years ago!

## Location, Location Location!

Sea sponges only get one chance to pick their homes once they mature, because they will live their entire adult lives in the same spots on the ocean floor.

# Whale Tale

It's amazing, but true: Some whales are even larger than the biggest dinosaurs were. Whales have lived on Earth for about 50 million years. As their food supply increased, whales ate more and became bigger over time.

## Air Head

Looking at a whale, you wouldn't think it has a nose—but it does. Over millions of years of evolution, whales' nostrils moved to the top of their heads, allowing them to breathe by surfacing, rather than by sticking their whole heads out of the water.

## Blow Up

When a whale comes to the surface and exhales, water in the blowhole and moisture in the whale's breath burst into the air in a marvelous spout. Because whales have differently shaped blowholes, they have differently shaped spouts.

## ROCK HEAD

Many whales do not have completely smooth skin. They are covered with barnacles, worms, lice, and colorful algae. Barnacles grow thickly on gray whales, giving them the appearance of a rocky surface.

On the right whale, there is a distinctive patch of barnacles, worms, and lice called a bonnet or rock garden. The head accounts for 25% of the whale's entire length.

# Filter Feeders

It may seem odd, but there are 10 kinds of whales that don't have any teeth at all. Hanging from their upper jaws are rows of bristled strands called baleen. Made of material similar to the human fingernail, the baleen acts as a food filter.

## BIG HEAD

Gray whale skull

Some whales have very large heads compared to the rest of their bodies. Their necks are stiff to keep their large heads steady while they're swimming. For this reason, most whales cannot turn their heads from side to side.

# Buddy System

You can often count on finding clown fish with grasslike sea anemones. Unlike most sea life, the clown fish is safe from the anemone's stinging cells because of a thick, slimy mucus on its body.

Sea anemones sting and eat fish that swim too close to its tentacles—except for clown fish, of course!

Sea anemones are closely related to jellyfish and coral. Anemones spend most of their time attached to coral reefs or on rocks at the bottom of the sea.

SEA ANEMONES

CLOWN FISH live in groups led by a dominant female. All clown fish are born male but have the ability to change their sex. If the dominant female dies, the dominant male will become female. Once the change is made, that fish cannot go back to being male.

# CLOWN FISH

Widely known as the clown fish, this sea creature is also called a clown anemonefish because of its close relationship with the sea anemone. Clown fish have a mutualistic relationship with sea anemones. The clown fish benefit from making their homes among the anemones, gaining protection from predators that stay away from the anemones' sting. In return, clown fish help to clean the anemones by picking off pesky parasites. The anemones will occasionally get to eat some of the food brought back by the clown fish.

# Echinoderms

Sea urchins, sand dollars, and sea lilies all belong to the phylum Echinodermata, a group of invertebrates that also includes sea stars and sea cucumbers. Nearly all echinoderms have something called radial symmetry, which means they have appendages, or limbs, extending out from a central point—just like spokes on a bicycle wheel! Sea cucumbers are one of the relatively few echinoderms that do not have noticeable radial symmetry.

**Sea cucumber**

SEA URCHINS MOSTLY EAT ALGAE AND SMALL ANIMALS LIVING ON THE SEABED AT THE BOTTOM OF THE OCEAN.

## Sea Urchins

A sea urchin's mouth is called Aristotle's lantern, named after the Greek philosopher, Aristotle, who first described it. The mouth of a sea urchin is surrounded by five toothlike plates that are strong enough to chew through stone!

**Sea urchin's mouth**

# Sea Lilies

Sea lilies and feather stars are part of a group of echinoderms called crinoids. Sea lilies resemble flowers with their long stalks and feathery arms. A sea lily stays permanently fixed to the seafloor, but it can shed the end of its stalk and use its arms to move away to escape predators. Feather stars mostly live on coral and have the ability to swim.

The word "echinoderm" comes from Greek words meaning "spiny skin." Many of the approximately 7,000 echinoderm species are covered in spiny skin. The sea urchin is a round sea animal completely covered in spines.

# Sand Dollars

Sand dollars that wash up on the beach look white, with a five-pointed star shape on their backs. These are actually the exoskeletons, or outer skeletons, of sand dollars that are no longer alive. Live sand dollars are covered in tiny, colorful spines, usually green, purple, or blue.

# Fun Facts about Conches

A conch shell is a large spiral with spines that some scientists think are used for protection. Inside the shell, its head has two pairs of tentacles. One pair has eyes on the end and the smaller pair gives the conch the ability to smell and touch.

Conches aren't just pretty shells you can find on the beach. They are actually sea-dwelling mollusks. Most true conch species are extinct now, but there are at least 60 species left, found mostly in the Indo-Pacific or Caribbean region. The queen conch can be found in warm tropical waters.

A conch moves by hopping. It pushes its foot against the floor, which makes the shell rise up and be thrown forward.

The animal inside the shell is a very popular dish in some countries. It can be eaten raw in a salad or cooked in a fritter, chowder, or gumbo, or even as a burger!

# Pair Matching

## Conch Connections

Draw a line to connect each conch shell on the left with its match on the right.

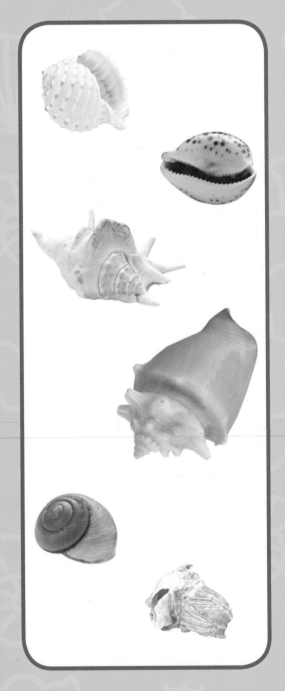

# Eels

In ancient times, people thought that eels were related to snakes and worms. Eels, however, are true fish with fins and gills and scales. Many swim in both salt and fresh water, something most fish can't do. The most common eels are anywhere from 1½ to 6 feet long and live in lakes, river bottoms, harbors, and marshes.

## Fire Mouths

Dragon moray eels have such long teeth that they can't close their mouths! The moray eel's wide mouth is filled with razor-sharp teeth, which help it tightly grip its prey.

## Slippery as an Eel

Eels have more mucus than most fish. That might make an eel feel good, but it makes touching one a pretty slimy experience. This spotted spoon-nose eel is one of about 600 species of eels.

# Irritable Eel

The "rattlesnake of the sea" is the moray eel, a fish that is as vicious as it looks. There are many types of morays hiding in the nooks and crannies of coral reefs. Some are large, reaching up to 10 feet and weighing 200 pounds. And some are poisonous—as if strong jaws, sharp teeth, and a powerful bite weren't enough.

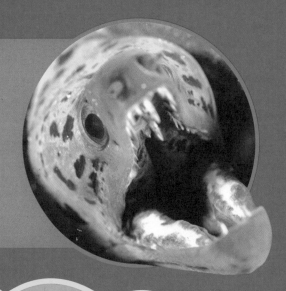

## Eel Garden

What looks like a question mark, lives in colonies, and acts like a real stick-in-the-mud? The garden eel. Garden eels spend all their time stuck tail-first in holes on the ocean floor. They rarely leave their burrows, and if danger comes, they sink right in up to their eyeballs. As many as 1,000 may live together.

## THE SHOCKING TRUTH

The electric eel is a 6-foot-long fish that swims in the rivers of South America. Most of its body is filled with special battery-like organs. A short blast of its electricity can stun a man and paralyze or kill small prey.

# City of Coral

One of the most colorful and populated areas of the sea is in and around a coral reef. The bright colors of the coral are caused by algae that live inside. Outside the coral, schools of tropical fish dazzle the eye with an equally fascinating display of color.

## It's Alive!

Coral may look and feel stony, but it is not rock. It's the skeleton of a living animal called a polyp. The polyps grow a skeleton on the outside to protect and support their soft bodies. Because the reef-building corals cannot live in water colder than 64°F, they are found only in warmer waters.

## Feeding Time

All animals have to eat, including coral polyps. How do they do it when they are attached to the ocean floor? Coral polyps actually have tiny arms that catch plankton and pass it into their mouth.

# Three Reefs

Reefs grow in different ways. A fringing reef is attached to the shore. An atoll, like the one shown at right, is a ring of coral formed around a sunken volcano. A barrier reef has a channel of water between it and the shore. Australia's Great Barrier Reef is a whopping 1,250 miles long.

## Know Your Coral

Stony corals, or hard corals, such as brain corals, form reefs. Gorgonians, or soft corals, such as sea fans, grow on the seafloor and on reefs, and look a lot like ferns or bushes.

## CORAL POPULATION

Every coral reef has a population consisting of thousands of different animals that live and thrive there—including shellfish, moray eels, sea horses, and sharks.

# Jawless Fish

Hagfish and lampreys are ancient relatives of true fish. They are eellike, scaleless, and jawless. Their round mouths look like suction cups lined with sharp keratin "teeth," and they're used to suck blood and body fluids out of other fish.

Some species of lampreys, called blood-feeding lampreys, are parasites that clamp onto prey, scrape their flesh, and suck their blood. Other species of lamprey don't eat at all as adults.

Like salmon, lampreys migrate to freshwater rivers to spawn. The female lamprey lays up to 300,000 eggs which will hatch into larvae. The larvae stay in the river for three to five years before traveling back to the ocean. After spawning, the lampreys die, since their digestive organs degenerate.

Lamprey was considered a delicacy, or especially delightful food, by the Romans, Vikings, and medieval Britons. Hagfish have recently become a food source due to overfishing of more popular fish.

Hagfish eat dead animals they find in the water, and they are able to go months without food. Hagfish can absorb nutrients through their skin.

If a hagfish feels threatened, it will squirt slime from the pores on the sides of its body. The slime expands in the water and can clog the gills of the predator, making the hagfish a fish to avoid!

# Keys to Communicate

Fish can't talk, but they can still send all kinds of different signals. Depending on the type of fish, they might make noise, flare out their gills, flash colors, or release smelly chemicals to tell other fish something's going on. Some fish, like this oscar, can even change colors to back out of a fight.

## Hello, My Name Is...

Dolphins can communicate with each other from birth using squawks, whistles, clicks, and squeaks. Dolphins call each other by "names"—specific sounds for different dolphins.

Dolphins communicate with body language: They leap into the air, slap their tails on the water, butt heads, and snap their jaws!

# BLADDER DRUM

Sea robins don't exactly sing, but they can make lots of noise. These fish make croaking and barking sounds using special muscles that vibrate the walls of their swim bladders.

## Smelly Delivery

Fish can use scents to send messages. When a predator bites a carp, the carp's skin releases a special chemical that tells nearby fish to swim away!

## Let's Talk

Piranhas make three different sounds to communicate with other fish, depending on what they are doing. They bark when confronting each other but aren't fighting, make a soft drumlike beat when chasing each other, and softly croak when they are fighting and biting each other.

WOOF WOOF WOOF

# Sea Horses

The odd and beautiful sea horse has a head like a delicate horse, a grasping tail like a monkey, an outer skeleton like an insect, and a pouch like a kangaroo. With all these borrowed parts, the sea horse doesn't look or act much like a real fish. Still, the tiny sea horse is a true fish.

## ALL BONES

The sea horse has bones inside and out. It has an inner skeleton like all bony fish, and an outer skeleton of bony plates. When a sea horse dies and dries out, its skeleton keeps its shape. People are so fascinated by the appearance of this odd fish that dried sea horses are used in ornaments and jewelry.

## Seaweed Sea Horse

Sea horses can change color to match their surroundings, but the award for best camouflage goes to the leafy sea dragon from Australia. It has amazing skin flaps that make it look much more like seaweed than a sea horse.

## Helpful Tail

Most fish swim with the aid of their tails, but not the sea horse. Its tail is long and thin and has no fin—it's more like a hand than a tail. The sea horse coils its tail into a tight spiral, grabbing onto seaweed and coral where it can stay still for hours. Sometimes two sea horses lock tails and have a tug-of-war.

# Eyes Apart

The sea horse's eyes work independently of each other. One eye can look forward to see what's coming, while the other looks backward to see what's behind. It's hard to hide from a sea horse.

## Swimming Motion

A sea horse swims like the leader of a very dignified parade. Vibrating its barely noticeable fins like mad—as fast as 35 times a second—the sea horse seems to grandly glide by.

Baby sea horses are born as fully developed miniatures of their parents. The female deposits her eggs in the male's kangaroo-like pouch and goes on her way. He carries the eggs for about six weeks until the babies—as many as 200—emerge.

## VACUUM SYSTEM

The sea horse eats with its long, tubelike snout which has a tiny trap door at the end. Whoosh! The snout vacuums up tiny forms of sea life. Click! The trap door closes. The sea horse may not have any teeth, but it does have a horse's appetite.

## STRING BEAN

A pipefish is not a sea horse that's been stretched or starved. It's just a skinny relative of the sea horse.

# Calico Creatures

## Calico Bass

The calico bass, also known as the kelp bass, is found on the Pacific coast of the United States from Oregon to Baja California. It is a very popular fish for recreational fishers in Southern California.

Calico bass eggs are usually found in kelp forests before they hatch. After they hatch, they stay hidden in the kelp for protection. As they age, the calico bass will move deeper into the ocean.

## CALICO BOX CRAB

The calico box crab, also called the leopard crab, is 2 to 4 inches long and gets its name from its gray or pale yellow shell with red patches. This unique coloring helps the crab blend in with the sandy areas in shallow water where it buries itself to hide.

CALICO CRABS ARE SCAVENGERS AND FEED ON THE DECOMPOSING MATTER OF PLANTS AND ANIMALS. THIS MAKES THEM A VERY IMPORTANT PART OF THE "GARBAGE DISPOSAL" COMMUNITY OF THE SEA. THEY ARE ALSO A VERY IMPORTANT PART OF THE KEMP'S RIDLEY SEA TURTLE'S DIET.

# Word Search

## Marine Animals

Look at the puzzle below and see if you can find the names of these marine animals. Circle the words going across, up and down, and diagonally. Some words may be backwards!

CALICO CRAB
CALICO BASS
HERMIT CRAB
BLOBFISH
GUITARFISH

SEA STAR
MANTA RAY
ATLANTIC SEA RAVEN
GUMMY SHARK
GREATER SOAPFISH

```
A T L A N T I C S E A R A V E N O P
D B D F Y E N I L O G N A P V O K G
D G T P C E M O T A R T H R T H G U
A N A L E T C B R G E H A M I S A I
X M H E R M I T C R A B D L E I K T
H K A C A E A G G H T Y R O K F L A
C W D N E B A Y I U E O K B U B Y R
A C B R T P E D I B R I O T A O R F
L Y L H P A T R N C S F R I W L U I
I K B I R R R H S A O E Q S R B M S
C S F N V A G A A B A L A O T A M H
O O N O B O M R Y E P D L S I E Y P
C D Q B S A U Z K Z F B E Y T F S H
R K I I F F S S O B I J F R G A H S
A Q C A L I C O B A S S B V U C R A
B M A B G U M M Y S H A R K T R A Q
```

# Giant Squids

The first time scientists were able to film a live giant squid was in 2006 near the Ogasawara Islands. They captured a 24-foot-long female squid and filmed her, allowing the world to see a living giant squid for the first time.

Giant squids mostly eat fish, shrimp, and other squids, but scientists think that they also attack and eat small whales.

When a giant squid is fully grown, it can be 33 feet long. The largest giant squid ever recorded was 59 feet long and weighed almost 1 ton!

The giant squid has the biggest eyes of any living creature. A giant squid's eyes can be 10 inches in diameter, which is the size of a beach ball. These large eyes help it see things deep in the ocean that other animals wouldn't be able to detect.

Giant squids can catch prey from up to 33 feet away by shooting out their feeding tentacles, which are covered with hundreds of sharp suckers.

# So Jelly

## Bell-y Dance

The body of a jellyfish is also known as a bell. A jellyfish moves through water by opening and closing its bell. Opening the bell allows it to fill with water, and closing it forces the water out and pushes the jellyfish forward.

## Not a Fish

A jellyfish is a mass of jellylike material with a mouth at its center and tentacles to gather food. It's not even close to being a fish!

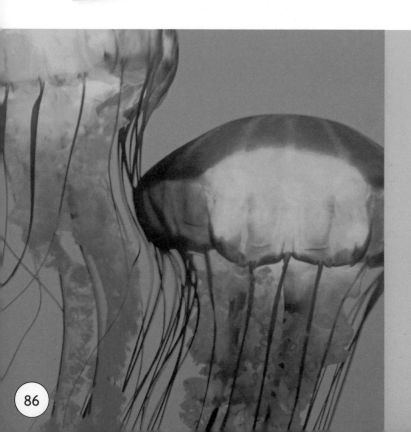

Jellyfish will evaporate in the sun because they are 98% water.

Despite their names and similar appearances, jellyfish and comb jellies are not so closely related. Jellyfish belong to the phylum Cnidaria, while comb jellies are part of the phylum Ctenophora. Comb jellies do not sting like jellyfish.

## Berry Sticky

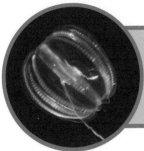

Sea gooseberries are comb jellies with a pair of sticky tentacles that help to capture prey.

## Rowing Rainbow

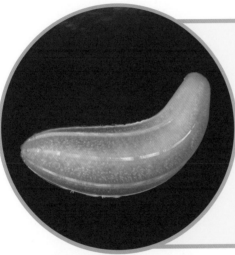

Comb jellies are named for the plates of comblike cilia that run up and down their bodies in rows. These combs work like tiny oars, beating back and forth to move the comb jellies through the water. The rows of combs in comb jellies diffract, or scatter, light to produce a beautiful rainbow effect.

Comb jellies are some of the earliest metazoans, or animals with multiple cells.

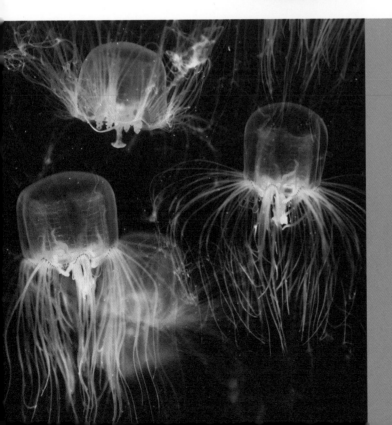

The box jellyfish, also known as a sea wasp, is the world's most venomous jellyfish, capable of killing humans with its sting.

# Great Barrier Reef

The Great Barrier Reef is one of the seven natural wonders of the world! It consists of around 2,900 individual reefs off the coast of Australia's Queensland. This magnificent reef is the largest structure on the planet made by living organisms. It is visible from outer space!

WHO LIVES HERE?

Thousands of mollusks exist throughout the Great Barrier Reef. Clams, oysters, octopuses, nudibranchs, and nautiluses make their homes among the coral.

The Great Barrier Reef is home to a wide array of sea creatures, including over 1,500 species of fish! Clown fish, parrot fish, butterfly fish, and surgeonfish are just a few!

Clown fish

Over 100 species of sharks and rays can be found here. The whitetip reef shark is one of the most common sharks in the Great Barrier Reef. Hammerhead sharks can also be seen in the reef, as can the more aggressive tiger shark.

Whitetip reef shark

Humpback whale

A large proportion of the global dugong population lives in the reef. This species is protected by law in Australia. Humpback whales and bottlenose dolphins are among the other marine mammals living in the reef.

Coral polyps attach themselves to rocks on the ocean floor, then divide into thousands of clones, or identical polyps. These colonies expand over time into reefs.

# Family Dynamics

## SAFE CIRCLE

For almost all animals, there is safety in numbers, especially when it comes to the young. When penguin chicks are strong enough, both parents head for the sea. The chicks group together in a crèche, or nursery, where they're less likely to be attacked by predators.

## MALE DUTY

As soon as eggs are laid, the female Adélie penguin heads for the sea to find food. The male stays with the eggs. By the time the Adélie female returns, the male hasn't eaten for about two weeks. Then it's his turn to eat while she stays with the eggs.

## THE GOOD MOTHER

Although sharks do not care for their babies after they have come into the world, mothers will search out safe places, called nurseries, where they can lay eggs or give birth. The Port Jackson shark mother seems especially attentive to finding a safe place for her eggs. Scientists think she carries them around in her mouth after laying them, looking for a reef crevice in which to lodge them for safe hatching.

Port Jackson shark egg

## Angel Baby

Newly hatched angelfish are stuck to their spawning places by fine, sticky thread attached to their heads. If a baby does break free, a parent swoops down to put it back with the others. However, after about three or four days, the babies bust loose in bunches too large to lasso. Soon, the full-grown angelfish are ready to raise fry, or young fish, of their own.

Spotted cat shark

## Tough Pups

A baby shark is called a pup, but it doesn't lead a dog's life. Its mother doesn't feed it or give it hunting lessons. In fact, grown sharks are happy to make a meal of tender babies. To survive, many young sharks go close to shore to grow up on their own. There are small fish to feed on there and no large sharks around.

## Foothold

King penguins have territories rather than nests. They incubate an egg standing up, and the spot where they stand is theirs. The sea is close to their colony, so parents eat and return often.

91

# Rainbow Connection

## Having a Blast

Triggerfish eat crabs and worms. To dig out these creatures, they will flap their fins to move sand and rocks and blast their prey with water from their mouths.

Yum Yum!

Triggerfish are not friendly. They will attack and charge at humans and other fish that come near their nests.

## Eye See You

The peacock mantis shrimp's eyes can see in two directions at once. Peacock mantis shrimp can see colors that humans can't!

Fairy basslets, also known as royal grammas, swim upside down under ledges and overhangs in the coral reefs where they live. Fairy basslets only grow up to 3 inches.

## Got Male

Parrot fish can change gender multiple times throughout their lives. If the dominant male in a school dies, one of the females will change genders and color and become the new dominant male.

The parrot fish eats algae that it gets from coral. To get the algae, it rips chunks of coral from the reef and grinds them up in its throat. This way it can eat the algae-filled polyps inside.

# Sea Turtles

Sea turtles can be found in oceans all over the world.

Most sea turtles are endangered, which means that they are in danger of becoming extinct or disappearing from the wild and captivity. This is due to a number of factors, including poaching, or illegal hunting and capturing, accidental capture by fishing gear, pollution, and climate change.

Unlike most other sea turtles, adult green sea turtles are herbivores. This means they eat only plants like sea grass and algae.

**DID YOU KNOW?**

Green sea turtles can live up to 80 years or more!

Female sea turtles lay 100 to 200 round eggs in the sand. The eggs hatch about two months later, and the baby turtles instinctively head towards the sea.

## Logging Miles

The loggerhead turtle is named for its large head and strong jaw, which helps it to crush prey with hard shells.

An adult female loggerhead sea turtle will often return to her natal beach, the beach where she was hatched, to lay her own eggs. She may have to travel thousands of miles to get there!

# FUN FACTS about
# LEATHERBACK SEA TURTLES

Leatherback sea turtles are the biggest turtles in the world. They can grow to around 7 feet long and weigh 500 to 2,000 pounds!

Leatherback sea turtles have been around for a long time—around 100 million years. They were alive when dinosaurs roamed the earth!

While most other sea turtles have hard shells, the leatherback's shell is somewhat flexible. As its name suggests, the leatherback's shell feels like leather and is almost rubbery to the touch.

# Special Features

Seabirds are pretty magnificent creatures: They spend a great deal of time at sea, and they can skillfully fly, float, dive, and swim. To maintain their lifestyles of great heights and deep dives, some seabirds have evolved extra physical adaptations.

## Ray Ban

Ultraviolet (UV) light means sunburn to humans. It's a range of colors many birds can see, but humans cannot. Very few seabirds are able to see UV light, and scientists think this is due to built-in "sunglasses" made up of tiny oil droplets that filter out the dangerous UV rays. Imagine never worrying about losing your sunglasses—it must be nice!

## COOL SHADES

It's no coincidence that many seabirds have unremarkable plumage, or feathers, that is dark on top and light on the bottom. This coloration is called countershading, and it helps to camouflage the birds from predators above and potential prey below.

# EARNING MILES

The sooty shearwater makes one of the longest and most impressive migrations of any animal on Earth. Each year, the New Zealand seabirds journey across the Pacific Ocean from the Arctic to the Antarctic. They have developed a figure-eight route that allows them to reach each pole for its respective summer, when there will be plenty of prey available.

## AIRBAGS ARE JUST FOR CARS, RIGHT?

Nature tells us otherwise. Gannets have inflatable air sacs under their skin that help to cushion them upon impact with the sea.

## Air Ways

In order to avoid getting their nostrils stuffed with saltwater when they plunge-dive into the ocean at high speeds, gannets breathe through slits located between the upper jaw and the head. A flap of hard tissue covers the slits and closes when the gannet dives.

# Baleen Whales

Baleen whales eat by taking in a mouthful of water and then spitting it out. Anything too large to squeeze through the baleen, such as krill, anchovies, sardines, and herring, is left behind to be swallowed.

Gray whales do not gulp their food. Instead, they swim to the bottom of the sea and lie on their sides. There they scoop up a mouthful of mud and then force it back out through their baleen. What's left behind is a dinner of crabs and clams.

**SUPER SCOOPERS**

## Krill-A-Plenty

Many baleen whales feed on krill—orange sea creatures that look like shrimp and grow up to 2 inches long. Scientists estimate that there may be 6½ billion tons in the Antarctic Ocean alone! A blue whale eats 4 tons of krill every day.

## Gulping Goodies

Fin whales, as well as blue, Bryde's, humpback, sei, and minke whales, are specially equipped to take huge gulps of krill and fish at one time. On their throats, there are grooves, or pleats, that stretch to allow the throat to expand.

## Bubble Trouble

Humpback whales prefer fish to krill, so they eat in a manner called bubble-net feeding. The humpback blows air from its blowhole to form a "net" as it swims in a spiral below a school of fish. The net of bubbles surrounds the fish so the whale can swim inside and trap its dinner. The humpback also feeds by lunging into a school of fish that it's herded into a ball.

# Tough Tusks

Walruses are easy to recognize by their long tusks and whiskers! These marine mammals can be found near the Arctic Circle. They have plenty of blubber to keep them warm in the cold ocean, and they have the ability to slow their heart rates so they can stay underwater for nearly 10 minutes without coming up for air.

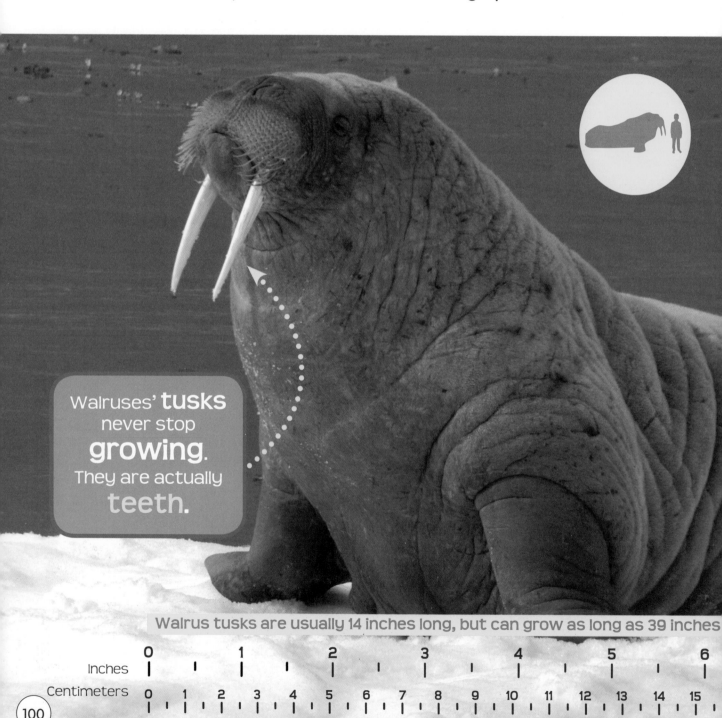

Walruses' **tusks** never stop **growing**. They are actually **teeth**.

Walrus tusks are usually 14 inches long, but can grow as long as 39 inches

Inches    0    1    2    3    4    5    6

Centimeters    0    1    2    3    4    5    6    7    8    9    10    11    12    13    14    15

Mother walruses keep their **babies** **safe** from crowds of walruses by putting them up on **rocks** and **ice floes.**

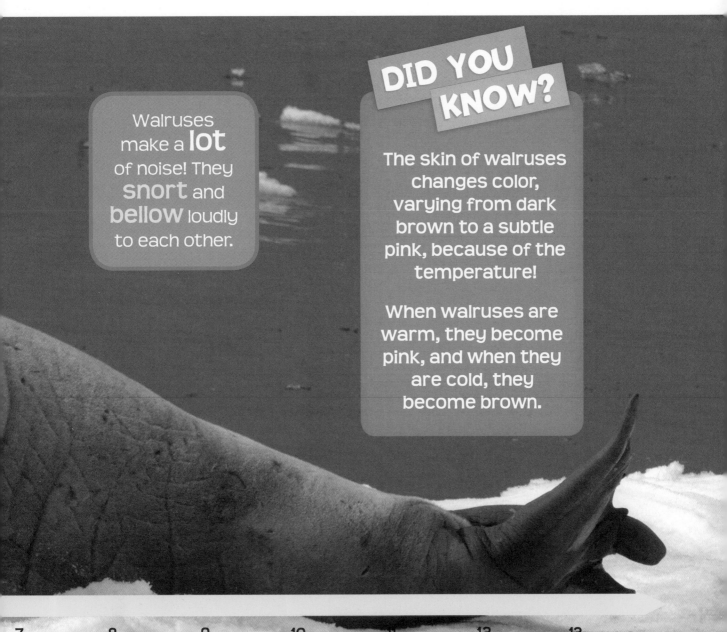

Walruses make a **lot** of noise! They **snort** and **bellow** loudly to each other.

## DID YOU KNOW?

The skin of walruses changes color, varying from dark brown to a subtle pink, because of the temperature!

When walruses are warm, they become pink, and when they are cold, they become brown.

7     8     9     10     11     12     13

18   19   20   21   22   23   24   25   26   27   28   29   30   31   32   33   34   35

# Shrimp

Even though the 2,000 known shrimp species vary widely in appearance, they all have the same bodily characteristics. A shrimp's body is divided into two parts, the head and the thorax, which are connected by a narrow abdomen and the cephalothorax.

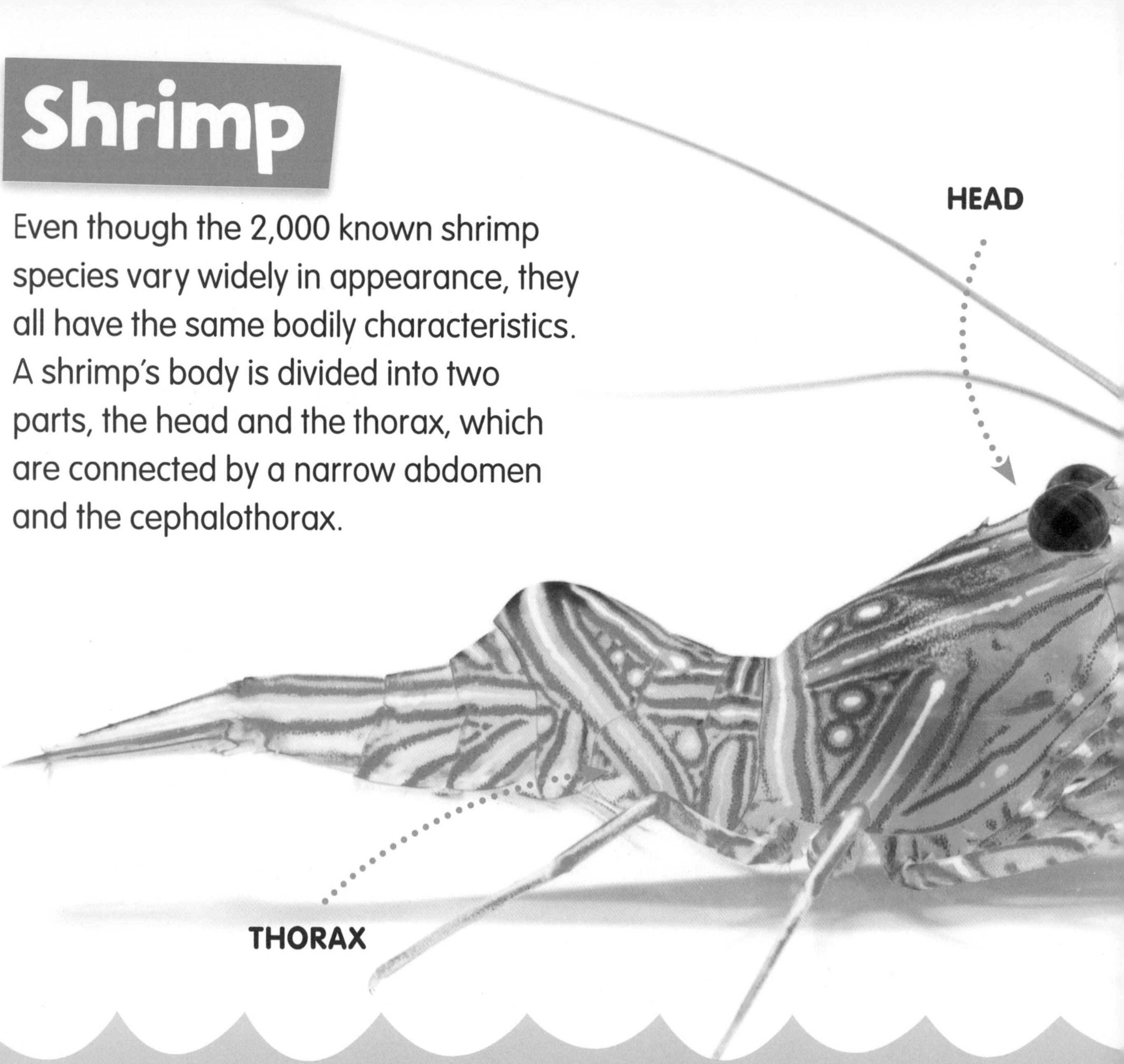

HEAD

THORAX

## Best of Both Worlds

Shrimp are able to live in both saltwater and freshwater environments. They are most commonly found in relatively shallow waters along coasts and in estuaries, which are places where a freshwater stream or river meets an ocean, where they can find plenty of food.

Shrimp can survive in water up to **16,000 feet deep!**

ONE SHRIMP CAN LAY UP TO
**1 MILLION EGGS**
AT A TIME. THESE EGGS ONLY TAKE
**TWO WEEKS** TO HATCH.

To protect itself from predators, the shrimp has a **sharp beak** called a **rostrum**. The rostrum helps to stabilize the shrimp when it is swimming backwards and forwards.

I'm fully grown!

## Safety in Numbers

Since shrimp are so small, ranging in size from 1/10 inch to 2 inches. They travel, breed, and eat in schools. This helps protect them from predators.

# Sluggish

There are over 3,000 species of nudibranchs. They vary in size from ¼ inch to 12 inches and can weigh up to 3⅓ pounds.

## You Are What You Eat

The nudibranch doesn't have any bones in its body and oozes slime, which can sometimes be poisonous. Whether a slug is poisonous depends on what it eats. Some nudibranchs absorb toxins from their prey and use them to ward off predators.

## Live to Eat

Sea slugs spend their days crawling around hunting for coral, sponges, and fish eggs, which they eat with their curved teeth.

# Background Blending

Even though nudibranchs are often considered the **most beautiful animals,** there are a few species that **don't have any color.** This is probably to help them blend in with their surroundings.

# Naked Gills

Nudibranchs belong to the suborder Nudibranchia, which means "naked gills." The snails earned this name because of the horns and feathery gills on their backs.

# His and Hers

Nudibranchs are hermaphrodites, which means they have both **male** and **female** organs. They lay one to six egg masses in **counterclockwise spirals** that contain up to **2 million eggs each.**

# Mollusk Madness

Oysters and clams belong to a phylum of invertebrates called mollusks. There are over 100,000 known species of mollusks.

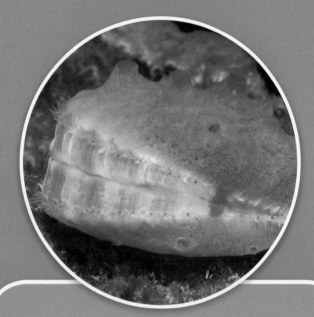

Believe it or not, scallops can swim! They squirt a jet of water out of their shells to help propel them forward.

Mussels, clams, oysters, and other bivalves make **great housekeepers!** They **filter** the water while searching for bacteria or phytoplankton to eat, and in the process they **remove pollutants** and **harmful waste** from the water.

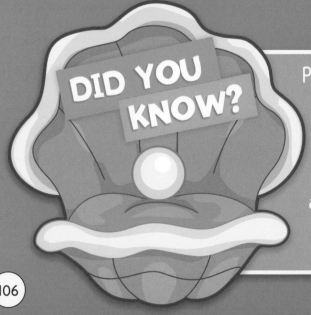

DID YOU KNOW?

Pearls are the only gemstones made by living creatures. When a foreign object, such as a parasite or particle of food, gets trapped in an oyster or other mollusk, the animal will begin coating the object with layers of a substance to defend itself against irritation. Over many years, the layers build up to form a pearl!

# Word Scramble

Unscramble the letters to find the names of some
amazing echinoderms and mollusks.

ESA CURNHI      _____

ADSN DLRALO      _____

ASE IYLL      _____

RATFEHE ARTS      _____

AES CMUCRUBE      _____

SOYRET      _____

SELSUM      _____

LSACLPO      _____

MLAC      _____

NHCNO      _____

# Betta Program

Betta fish are originally from Cambodia, Laos, Vietnam, and Thailand, and are also known as Siamese fighting fish. They don't get their name from the Greek alphabet, though: It comes from the Thai phrase *ikan betta*, which means "persistent fish."

## DID YOU KNOW?

BETTA FISH ARE NOT TECHNICALLY MARINE ANIMALS, BUT THEY DO LIKE SALT IN THEIR WATER.

## Bubble Nest

The male Siamese fighting fish builds a nest of bubbles on the water's surface. He carries each egg in his mouth and places it in the nest, which constantly needs new bubbles. When the babies fall out and escape faster than he can return them—and there's no time to repair the nest—Father knows his job is done.

# INTO THE LABYRINTH

Betta fish breathe air and can actually survive out of the water for short periods of time, as long as they are kept moist. They have a special organ called the labyrinth organ that lets them breathe air from the surface and survive in waters with low oxygen, such as rice paddies, stagnant ponds, and polluted water.

## Color Changes

Betta fish are popular pets because of their bright colors, but in the wild they are dull brown or green, except when they get agitated.

## PLAY NICE

Male betta fish are aggressive and territorial with each other and will often fight if put in the same tank. Female betta fish get along together, and male betta fish can be around other kinds of fish without issue.

# Talent Show

These close relatives of squids, octopuses, and nautiluses are masters of disguise and have abilities and adaptations humans can only imagine!

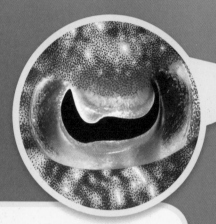

## SUPER VISION

Cuttlefish can see behind them and have incredible eyesight. They have "W"-shaped pupils that give them a large horizontal field of vision, as well as the ability to entirely reshape their eyes, much like we can change the size of our pupils to focus on different objects.

## Strolling Along

Cuttlefish babies and some cuttlefish species walk along the ocean floor instead of swimming. Scientists think that walking allows them to move around without traveling too far from a place to hide.

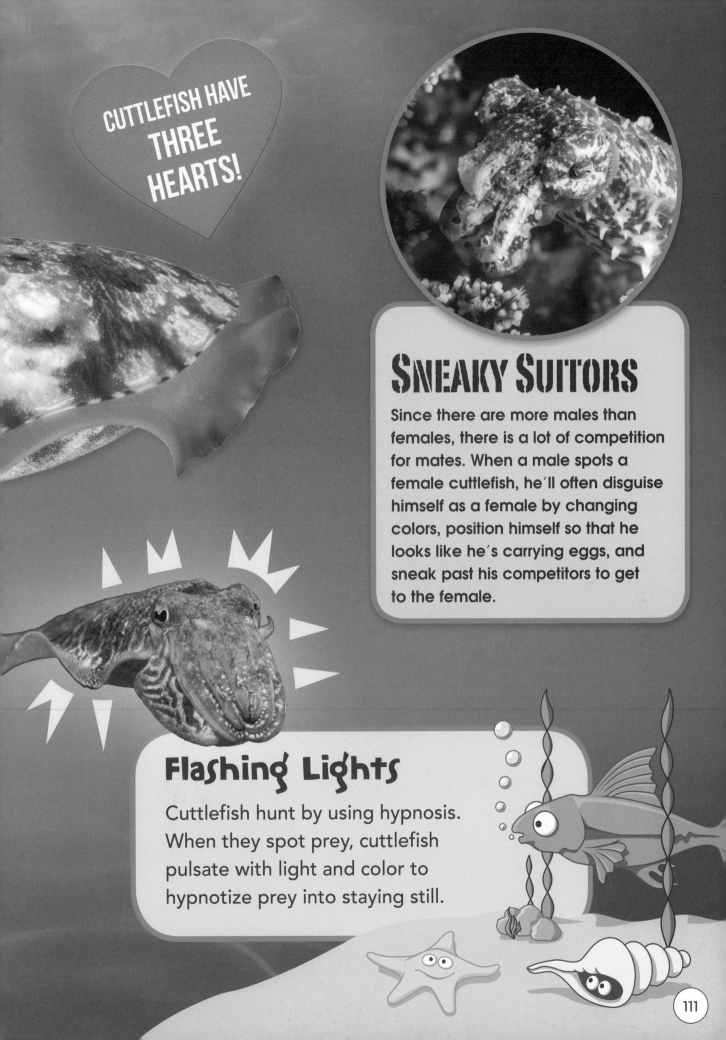

CUTTLEFISH HAVE **THREE HEARTS!**

# SNEAKY SUITORS

Since there are more males than females, there is a lot of competition for mates. When a male spots a female cuttlefish, he'll often disguise himself as a female by changing colors, position himself so that he looks like he's carrying eggs, and sneak past his competitors to get to the female.

# Flashing Lights

Cuttlefish hunt by using hypnosis. When they spot prey, cuttlefish pulsate with light and color to hypnotize prey into staying still.

# Cute Sea Creatures

## Otter-ly Furry

A sea otter has a lot more hair than a human! In a patch the size of a **fingernail**, an otter has **more hair** than a human has on her **whole head!**

## Shade Shifter

The color of a nudibranch depends on what it eats. When this sea slug eats, it absorbs the pigment, natural matter that gives living things color, of its prey and displays that color.

## Crack Down

Sea otters have pockets of skin on their arms where they store both shellfish snacks and the rocks they use to crack open their prey.

# Harboring Seals

The harbor seal is the most common seal and is found in cold, shallow waters in the polar regions.

## White Russian

Beluga whales get their name from the Russian word *bielo* which means "white," but these whales aren't born white. They are gray at birth, and it can take up to eight years before they are truly white.

## ALL IN THE FAMILY

Most whales are fairly social and like to live in groups. These herds, or pods, vary in number and consist of family members and friends. Beluga whales usually live in the Arctic Ocean or subarctic waters in large groups of up to 1,000. However, every few years one or two will follow cold currents as far south as New York City.

# Parrots of the Sea

The Atlantic puffin, known as the common puffin, has very similar coloring to a penguin. The most noticeable difference is the puffin's colorful beak, which has given it the nickname "sea parrot"!

## Super Divers

The Atlantic puffin's waterproof feathers allow it to stay warm underwater. Though puffins usually stay underwater for 20 to 30 seconds at a time, they are capable of diving 200 feet deep!

## DID YOU KNOW?

Puffins spend most of their time in the sea, but can also fly in the sky at up to 55 miles an hour— as fast as cars traveling on a highway!

# A Beak Full!

On average, a puffin will carry 10 fish at a time in its beak. Ridges on the puffin's tongue and spines on the roof of its mouth allow it to hold on to fish while it dives back into the ocean and opens its mouth to catch more food.

## Soul Mates

Puffins return to land for breeding season, on the coasts and islands in the North Atlantic Ocean. Puffins often choose mates for life, and the female will lay one egg per year. The male and female take turns incubating, or sitting on the egg until it hatches. Puffin couples will often make their way back to the same burrow each year to lay their eggs.

# Swim Fans

All snakes can swim, but there are some snakes that live mostly in the water. These reptiles are called—unsurprisingly—sea snakes. Though they may come up often for air, sea snakes can stay underwater for an hour or more!

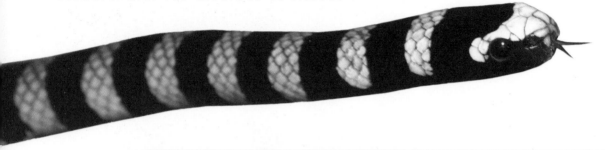

## Fish Food

Most sea snakes prefer to eat mainly fish, but the banded sea krait primarily feeds on eels. A banded sea krait can swallow an entire eel as big as the krait itself!

Eel

## On Land and at Sea

Unlike most other sea snakes, the banded sea krait is amphibious, meaning it can live on both land and water. It returns to land to mate, lay eggs, and digest food, spending up to 10 days at a time out of the water.

# Sea Snakes vs. Eels

Sometimes eels are mistaken for sea snakes, but there are some important differences between the two animals: Sea snakes have lungs and must come up for air in order to breathe, while eels breathe through their gills and remain underwater like fish. Sea snakes have scales, and eels usually have fins and no scales.

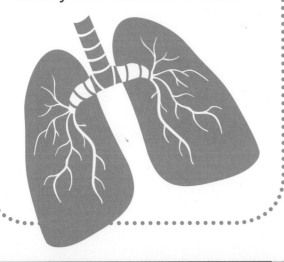

## Snake Bite

All sea snakes are poisonous. The beaked sea snake's venom is one of the deadliest poisons of all snakes! Luckily for humans, these snakes are not aggressive and are unlikely to attack people.

# WASHED ASHORE

The yellow-bellied sea snake is pelagic, meaning that it spends most of its life in the open waters of the ocean rather than in water close to land. These snakes will often float on the sea in huge groups. Unfortunately, yellow-bellied sea snakes occasionally wash up on the beach, likely due to stormy weather.

# Living Color

A fish of many colors! Of the over 80 species of angelfish that live in the sea, most species will change color as they age.

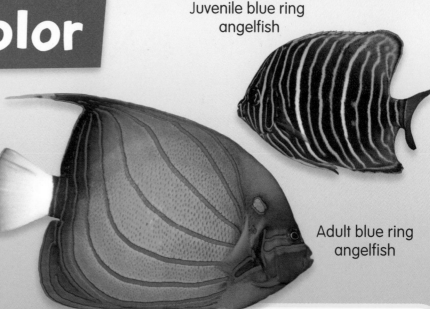

Juvenile blue ring angelfish

Adult blue ring angelfish

## AGING WELL

Looking at an adult and a juvenile blue ring angelfish side by side, you wouldn't be able to guess they were the same species! Juveniles are blue-black, with vertical blue and white stripes, while adults are orange-yellow with blue stripes.

## GOING FOR GOLD

French angelfish are born with black scales, and juveniles have three vertical yellow stripes. As the fish get older, the yellow bars fade and gold edges appear.

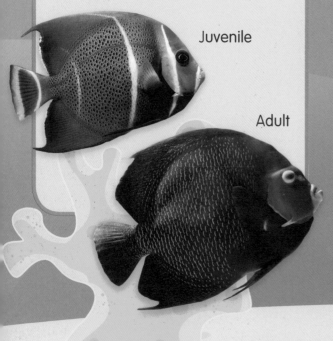

Juvenile

Adult

## Look-alikes

Gray angelfish are almost black when they are young, with yellow bands on each side, and are often confused with French angelfish. When they grow up, they are gray with dark spots on their scales. Gray angelfish are also known as pot covers!

Juvenile gray angelfish

# Housekeeping

Young French angelfish and gray angelfish work for their food as cleaner fish. They feed on loose scales and parasites of larger fish. This service is so popular that fish will line up to be cleaned!

## TOUGH GUYS

Gray angelfish have a reputation as the tough guys of the many angelfish species. They can live in the warm waters of the tropics, as well as the cold waters of New England.

## A Rare Breed

The striking queen angelfish is closely related to the blue angelfish. These two species are known to mate and form hybrids, a combination of species. This behavior is rare among angelfish.

## Your Majesty!

Queen angelfish get their royal name from the blue-ringed black mark on their heads that resembles a crown.

# All Smiles

Whose cute face is poking out of the water? It's a bottlenose dolphin, one of the most common and well-known types of dolphins. The shape of their mouths makes them look like they're always smiling.

Dolphins need to be **awake** to **breathe,** so they get their rest by letting **one half** of their **brains sleep** at a time.

The bottlenose dolphin can breach up to **15 feet high—** that's like jumping over a small tree!

**Female dolphins** are called **cows,** and **babies** are **calves. Males** are called **bulls.**

# Crack the Code
## Dolphinfish

The common dolphinfish is not related to dolphins at all. It is a large, colorful tropical fish that plays an important role in the ocean food chain. Dolphinfish eat squids, open ocean crustaceans, and small fish, and they are food for sharks and other large predators. These fish are iridescent and beautifully colored, often blue, green, and gold with black spots.

Fill in the blanks to find out the common dolphinfish's Hawaiian name and the name of its closest relative. Look at each letter below, and write the letter that comes before it in the alphabet in the space above.

M _ _ _ _ - _ _ _ _
  N B I J  N B I J

_ _ _ _ _ _ _ **DOLPHINFISH**
Q P N Q B O P

# Sea Grazers

Manatees and dugongs are often referred to as sea cows, because they are large, slow-moving mammals that graze on underwater grass and plants. However, they are much more closely related to elephants!

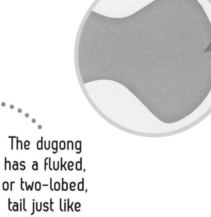

Manatee

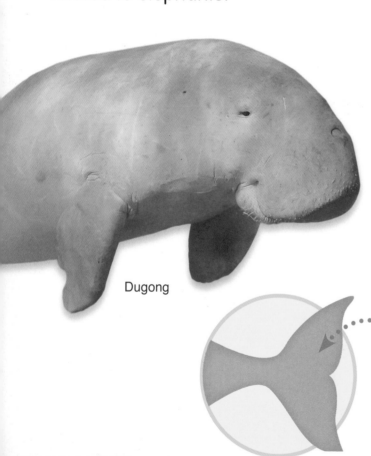

Dugong

The dugong has a fluked, or two-lobed, tail just like a dolphin.

Manatees have tails that look like paddles.

## GENTLE GIANTS

Manatees are gentle animals and have very few natural predators in the wild. Only sharks, crocodiles, and alligators will attack them. Dugongs may be preyed upon by sharks, killer whales, and saltwater crocodiles.

Some people believe that dugongs and manatees inspired stories about mermaids and mermen! Both manatees and dugongs frequently rise out of the water to breathe, and they can turn their heads, which may explain why they were mistaken for merfolk. During his first journey to the Americas, Christopher Columbus recorded a mermaid sighting of his own in his journal. In fact, he was looking at manatees!

## Going Solo

Dugongs are peaceful, often solitary animals. They tend to spend their time alone or in pairs, but herds of 100 dugongs sometimes gather together.

## Ocean View

Most manatees live in freshwater, but ocean-dwelling manatees live in coastal areas. The West Indian manatee moves between freshwater and salt water. Dugongs are closely related to manatees and only live in the sea.

# Commuters

Atlantic salmon

Spawning chum salmon

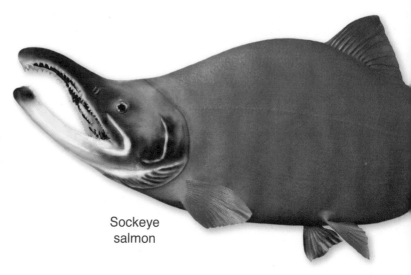

Sockeye salmon

## Fresh Paint

Different species of salmon can be different colors. For example, chum salmon are silvery-blue, while cherry salmon have bright red stripes. Most species of salmon, however, change color when they move from freshwater to live in the ocean. The sockeye salmon turns bright red when spawning, or laying eggs.

## EGG-CEPTIONAL

After traveling up to 1,000 miles in a single trip upriver, female salmon can lay more than 4,000 eggs. They will make depressions in the riverbed with their tails to lay eggs and cover them with mud after they are fertilized by a male.

## Short-lived

Pacific salmon will die after spawning, and 50% of all other salmon species will die a few weeks after spawning. The fish that survive will spawn two to three more times before dying.

## Yum

Young salmon eat mostly insects, plankton, and invertebrates. Adult salmon eat other fish, squid, eels, and shrimp.

## Long Distance Swimmer

Freshwater or salt water? There are a few unusual fish that can live in both. The salmon begins its spectacular journey in the freshwater river where it was born. At three years old and about 10 inches long, the fish starts downstream to the salty sea. After four or five years, and weighing up to 20 pounds, the salmon returns to spawn at the place where it was born. It struggles fiercely against the current, waterfalls, dams, and predators, arriving at its birthplace bruised and exhausted, but ready to reproduce.

# Amazing Rays

With its flat body and kite-like shape, it's hard to mistake the manta ray for just another fish. Unlike other rays, manta rays are found near the surface of the ocean. They are cousins to sharks, sharing the same type of skeleton.

## Cool Tool

A manta ray streaks through the water with two fleshy parts that stick out of its pectoral fins like horns. These horns act like scoops, channeling fish, plankton, and other food into the manta's great mouth.

THE ONLY OTHER SEA ANIMALS **BIGGER** THAN MANTA RAYS ARE WHALES AND SHARKS.

## *Mistaken Identity*

Manta rays are often thought of as dangerous because they are confused with stingrays.

## Cruise Control

The giant manta ray measures as much as 20 feet across and weighs up to 3,000 pounds. Unlike bottom dwellers, mantas cruise the water's surface eating small plant and animal organisms. Sometimes, by flapping its spectacular "wings," a manta ray can "fly" 15 feet out of the water.

# Skating By

Skates are usually flat, like rays, and have long tails. They live on the floor of the ocean so they can quickly burrow into the sand to avoid predators.

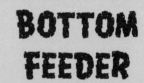

Spiracles

## BOTTOM FEEDER

A skate's mouth is on the bottom of its body, which allows it to search in the sand for food. In order to breathe, skates use spiracles, or gill slits behind the eyes, to pump water to the gills without swallowing sand.

## Egg Purse

The egg cases of a skate are often found on the beach. These cases are little black rectangles with strings. Long ago, people who found them thought they were left by mermaids. Even today, the skate's egg cases are called "mermaid's purses."

# NOT A SHARK

The guitarfish shows how closely related sharks and rays really are. It has a longer, thinner, more shark-like body, but its gills are on the underside of its body, so it's definitely a ray. The guitarfish's teeth are blunt, not sharp, but there are a lot of them—65 or 70 rows.

Stingray

## GET MOVING

Skates are members of the ray family. When they swim, they move their pectoral fins from front to back instead of flapping them like rays.

Pectoral fin

Skate

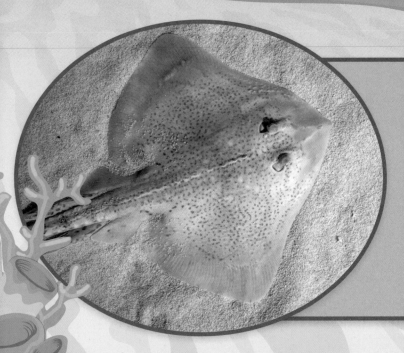

## Water Skate

What's that shadow gliding along the ocean floor? It's a skate—an animal belonging to a large branch of the ray family. It's shaped like a kite, and its fins seem to ripple as it swims. Eating fish, snails, and clams at the bottom of the sea, the skate can grow up to 6½ feet long and weigh up to 100 pounds.

# Flat as a Pancake

There are over 700 species of flatfish that live all over the globe. Most flatfish live near the bottom of the ocean. This is where they hunt for fish and small water animals to eat.

## SIDE TO SIDE

Since the flatfish lies with one side of its body facing the ground, its mouth opens differently from other fish. Instead of opening up and down, a flatfish's mouth opens side to side.

## MASTER OF DISGUISE

The flatfish is an expert at disguise. Some species will glide to the seabed and flap their fins to stir up mud and sand. This covers the fish's body and allows it to hide from predators. Other flatfish, like the peacock flounder, can change colors to blend into their surroundings.

# ONE-SIDED

The flounder's head fools you because two eyes are staring back at you, but both of the flatfish's eyes are on the same side of its head. A flatfish is born with eyes on both sides of its head, but as it grows, one eye will migrate to the other side of its head.

Many flatfish species live in **shallow coastal water**, but the **Pacific halibut** can go as deep as **3,000 feet.**

# BLENDING IN

The flatfish can have spots, circles, or dots on its head and body to help it blend into the ocean floor.

# Search & Find®

## Peacock Flounder Peek-a-Boo

Search & Find® these 5 different peacock flounders among the coral, seaweed, and other animals below.

Answers on page 306

# Feathers and Spines

## High Alert

A roosterfish has spines on its body that it can make stand up when it feels threatened or excited.

## DOUBLE DUTY

The feathery pectoral fins of a lionfish serve two purposes: The lionfish uses them to attract prey and to keep predators away.

## YIKES! SPIKES!

Porcupine fish are armed from head to tail with prickly spikes. Although many are camouflaged in drab colors, others are dotted and brightly marked, warning predators that they can be toxic.

# Sky High

## DIVE IN

To catch its prey, the common tern hovers over the water and plunge-dives to pluck its meal from the surface or below. The tern eats small fish, insects, crustaceans, and, occasionally, squids or other invertebrates. Terns are opportunistic predators and will steal prey from other terns, too.

## Thirst for Salt

If a common tern lives near the ocean, it will only drink salt water, even if there is freshwater nearby. Common terns drink water in a special way: They glide over the water and dip their bills into it several times.

## Baby Food

The tufted puffin can hold five to 20 fish in its bill at a single time. It brings the fish back to its nest for the chicks. The adult puffin eats its own meal while still underwater.

# Careful Eater

After a brown pelican catches its dinner, it needs to drain the water that it scooped up with the fish out of its pouch. It has to be careful, because gulls will often try to steal the fish right out of the pelican's pouch! They will even perch on the pelican's head to do it!

# Stand-up Job

The brown pelican uses the skin on its feet to keep its eggs warm by standing on them! This was a problem in the 1960s and 1970s, because a pesticide called DDT made the eggshells thinner, causing them to crack when the pelican stood on them. Since DDT was banned, the brown pelicans are back to normal.

# Burrow Deep

Tufted puffins build their nests in burrows that can reach a depth of 5 feet. They build these burrows in cliff edges and slopes, and occasionally under boulders, rock piles, or dense vegetation.

# Cats and Dogs

## Tracking Device

Hardhead catfish, also known as sea catfish or tourist trout, have six rounded barbels on their chins that look like whiskers. These barbels help them find shrimp, fish, and crabs to eat where they live.

## Sharp Cat

The hardhead catfish has dorsal and pectoral fins that are supported by a sharp, slime-covered spine. The catfish will hold the dorsal spine erect when it gets excited—it's so sharp that it can pierce the sole of a shoe!

## Dad on Duty

Hardhead catfish spawn in the spring. The male hardhead carries the eggs in his mouth until they are ready to hatch and the young fish can fend for themselves.

## A Dog's Life

The spiny dogfish got its name from fishermen who thought the small shark's habit of hunting in packs was similar to that of dogs. Spiny dogfish can form into groups of thousands!

Scientists believe that spiny dogfish can live between **20 and 75 years**! They develop very slowly, however. The female dogfish can be pregnant for **two years**!

## Food for Thought

Dogfish eat bony fish, octopuses, smaller sharks, squids, crabs, and shark egg cases. These small sharks are hunted by cod, red hake, goosefish, other spiny dogfish, larger sharks, seals, and orcas, despite having venomous spikes on each side of their dorsal fins.

## Dog of a Fish

Spiny dogfish, smooth dogfish, spotted dogfish, chain dogfish—dogfish sharks are a large, varied family, and their names prove it. Some even have more than one name: The lesser spotted dogfish is also called the small spotted catshark!

# Here Comes the Sun

The mola, also called the giant ocean sunfish, is the largest bony fish in existence. This fish can grow to weigh 5,000 pounds and be as long as 14 feet from head to tail and 10 feet from back to stomach!

## Break It Down

Molas have small mouths, so they have to suck in and spit out their food in order to feed. This process breaks the food into smaller pieces that the mola can more easily swallow.

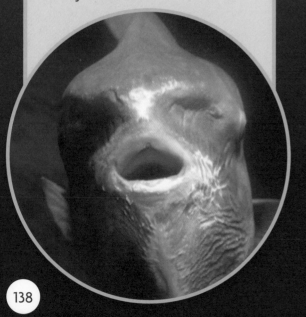

## Growth Spurt

A newly hatched mola is only $\frac{1}{10}$ inch long. A fully grown mola weighs over 60 million times as much as it did when it first hatched! Compare that to humans who normally only weigh about 30 times what they do at birth!

## I Got Sunshine

Molas like to sun themselves near the surface of the ocean, which is why they are called sunfish! People often mistake their dorsal fins sticking out of the water as they sun themselves for sharks.

## Steering Wheel

The mola has a funny appearance. Its round shape comes from its small tail, called a clavus. The clavus doesn't grow with the rest of the fish, staying short and rounded. The mola uses its clavus to steer itself.

## Sunny Outlook

Molas deal with skin parasites in several ways: One method is to swim to a place where smaller fish will eat the parasites off the molas. Another way molas remove parasites is by jumping out of the water and smacking themselves on the surface. Scientists think that molas sun themselves so that gulls will land on them and pick off the parasites. After one side is done, the mola flips over for the bird to repeat.

139

# Sail and Fly

Sailfish live all over the world in warm and temperate parts of the ocean. They get their name from their large dorsal fins, which stretch almost the whole length of their bodies and are taller than their bodies are thick!

## FLY GUYS

Flying fish have a streamlined torpedo shape that helps them gain enough speed to break the surface of the ocean, and wing-like fins that flap to get them airborne. Once in the air, the fish can reach a height of over 4 feet and travel up to 655 feet in a single glide!

Sailfish are very **large**, powerful fish. They can grow to be more than **10 feet long** and weigh up to **220 pounds!**

## Speed Demon

Widely considered the fastest fish in the sea, the sailfish has been clocked leaping as fast as 68 miles per hour.

## Round-up

Sailfish are usually found close to the surface of the ocean and far away from the land, where they can find sardines and anchovies. Sailfish herd the schools of fish with their sails, making them easier to catch.

# One of a Kind

The horseshoe crab is similar to an arthropod, meaning that it is more closely related to spiders, ticks, and scorpions than it is to true crabs. However, these crabs are in a class of their own, called Merostomata, which means "legs attached to the mouth."

Horseshoe crabs have many predators. Their eggs and larvae are eaten by birds and other ocean animals. Adult horseshoe crabs are eaten by sharks, sea turtles, and gulls, and killed by humans who use them as bait and fertilizer.

## High Tide

Horseshoe crabs live mostly in deep waters but will migrate in the spring to shallow waters. At night, they emerge to mate and lay eggs when the tide is high. A female horseshoe crab will lay 90,000 eggs every spring.

# Playing Parts

The horseshoe crab's body is divided into three sections. The first contains its mouth, a pair of feeding pincers, and five sets of legs. The second is the abdomen, which has five sets of gills used to breathe and swim upside down. The third is a tail spike, which it uses to steer and to right itself if it flips over while swimming.

# New Clothes

A horseshoe crab's exoskeleton doesn't grow as the crab does, which means that it needs to molt, or shed the exoskeleton and grow a new one, in order to develop. A horseshoe crab will molt 16 to 17 times before it reaches adult size.

# OLD FOLKS

The horseshoe crab is called a living fossil because it has been on Earth for about 220 million years and is nearly identical to its ancient ancestors. Horseshoe crabs were on the planet before dinosaurs!

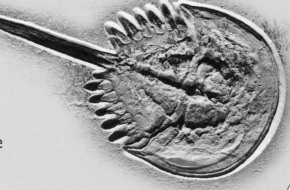

# Stand Out Sharks

The thresher shark and wobbegong shark are shark species with very unique appearances.

## Near and Far

Adult thresher sharks can be found both in coastal waters and far from the shore, in shallow and deep waters. Younger sharks stick mainly to shallow bays and closer to shore.

## FIN FRIGHT

A thresher shark is very easy to recognize. It has a gigantic, curving upper tail fin that can be as long as the shark's whole body! These sharks use their tails as a weapon to herd, stun, and kill their prey.

## Snack Time

Thresher sharks mainly eat schools of small fish, but they also snack on octopuses, squids, and other fish that live at the bottom of the ocean. Thresher sharks can jump out of the water and occasionally catch a seabird to eat.

# Fringe Benefits

The wobbegong shark, or "carpet shark," has a wide, flat body with dark lines and spots to help it camouflage itself on the ocean floor. The fringe around its mouth is made of nasal barbells and dermal lobes, which help the fish sense its surroundings.

## Killer Bite

Wobbegong sharks hide under reef ledges during the day, but at night they emerge to hunt on the reef. They perch on the reef until they spot prey, then lunge up and grab the prey with one powerful bite.

Wobbegong sharks produce eggs, which they keep inside their bodies until they are ready to hatch. They then give birth to live pups!

# Got Whale

## WHALE OF A HUNTER

The orca, or killer whale, is actually the largest of the dolphins. Orcas are fast, intelligent hunters that often work in a group. If they spot seals resting on ice floes, orcas may tip the ice, then catch the seals as they slide off.

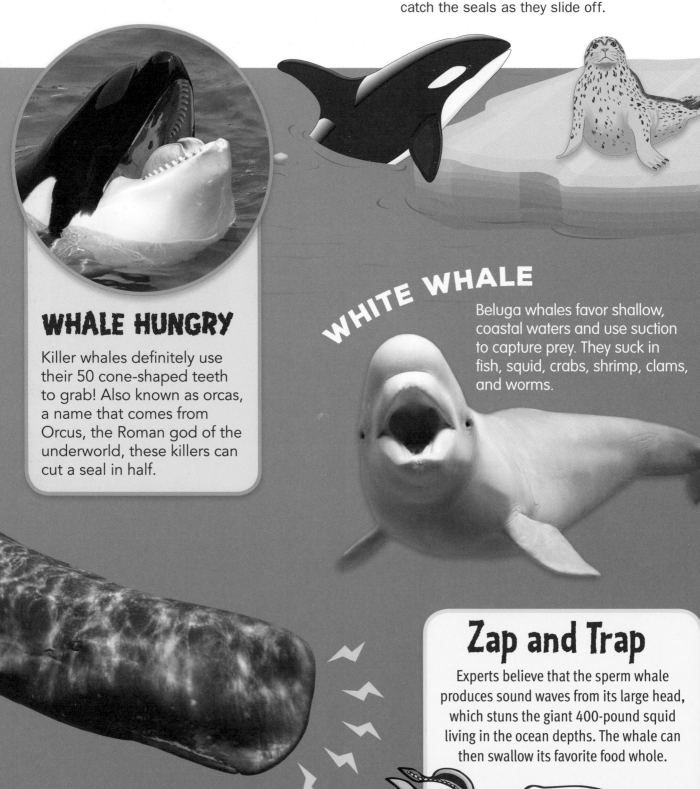

## WHALE HUNGRY

Killer whales definitely use their 50 cone-shaped teeth to grab! Also known as orcas, a name that comes from Orcus, the Roman god of the underworld, these killers can cut a seal in half.

## WHITE WHALE

Beluga whales favor shallow, coastal waters and use suction to capture prey. They suck in fish, squid, crabs, shrimp, clams, and worms.

## Zap and Trap

Experts believe that the sperm whale produces sound waves from its large head, which stuns the giant 400-pound squid living in the ocean depths. The whale can then swallow its favorite food whole.

# Word Search

## A Whale of a Word Search

Look at the puzzle below and see if you can find these words and names of animals in the whale family. Circle the words going across, up and down, and diagonally. Some words may be backwards!

BALEEN      HARBOR PORPOISE

ORCA      HUMPBACK WHALE

SPERM WHALE      BOTTLENOSE DOLPHIN

CETACEAN      ODONTOCETI

BELUGA WHALE      NARWHAL

```
B X H A R B O R P O R P O I S E D
D O D B Y E N I L O G N A P O R P
D C T B V B K O H H S T H R N E A
A E Z L E S E O D O N T O C E T I
X L G A L P G L Y W Q N D L S W K
H A W C H E A G U R N Y R L P S O
G H D K E R N Y I G Q A K I O R R
D W B R Y M S O T B A K R R U C K
A K L H P W T A S K B W J W Y E E
A C B I R H N H R E A O H G H T A
J A R N V A G A A K D L N A C A I
B B N O B L M R P N F O R R L C L
Y P Q B I E U Z E Z V A L Y Q E H
I M I T F F S E O B B J R P Q A K
R U E Y G X L K Y T B L B V H N A
A H C N E A C L O L T A O M P I B
O W A R B L E D W H E L A B T T N
```

# Sea Otters

These cute sea creatures live along the coastline of the Pacific Ocean in Asia and North America. They are specially adapted to living in the water, with ears and nostrils that close in the water, webbed feet, and water-repellent fur.

## Otter Bonding

Sea otters are social creatures, often found floating in groups called rafts. They will sometimes hold hands so they don't drift apart.

## Drop Anchor

Otters sometimes wrap themselves in kelp, a type of giant seaweed attached to the ground, when they go to sleep. This keeps them anchored in place.

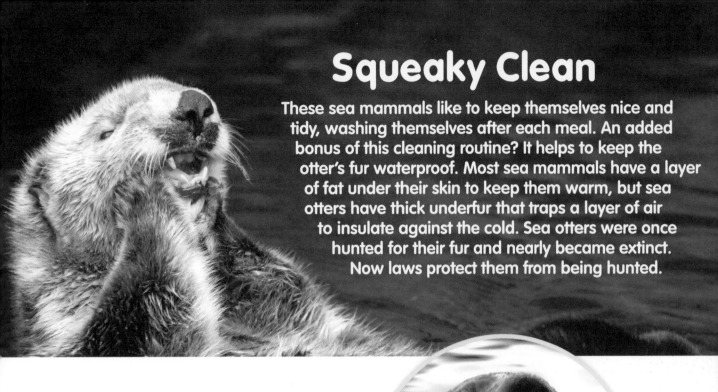

# Squeaky Clean

These sea mammals like to keep themselves nice and tidy, washing themselves after each meal. An added bonus of this cleaning routine? It helps to keep the otter's fur waterproof. Most sea mammals have a layer of fat under their skin to keep them warm, but sea otters have thick underfur that traps a layer of air to insulate against the cold. Sea otters were once hunted for their fur and nearly became extinct. Now laws protect them from being hunted.

## Cute and Clever

Otters can use simple tools like rocks to open shellfish or mussels to eat.

### DID YOU KNOW?

SEA OTTERS ARE PART OF THE WEASEL FAMILY!

## Baby on Board

Sea otters are the only otters to spend the majority of their lives in the water. They even give birth at sea! No other otter species does this. Mothers care for their young as they float on their backs, holding their babies on their chests.

## Gulls

### Lots of Laughs

If you visit a beach along the Atlantic Coast or Gulf Coast, you may notice some strange, high-pitched laughter. Those goofy laughs aren't coming from people—they are from birds called laughing gulls! A laughing gull's call sounds a lot like "ha, ha, ha!"

HA, HA, HA!

### Cleaning House

After an egg hatches, the male laughing gull will remove the eggshell from the nest. If pieces of eggshell remain, they can get stuck on top of an unhatched egg and prevent it from hatching.

### MEAN MACHINE

You don't want to get too close to kelp gulls when they are in breeding season. These birds will defend their nests by dive-bombing intruders with their wings, bill, or feet!

# Big Appetite

Gulls certainly aren't picky eaters! There are nearly 50 species of gulls, and, depending on the species, their diets include crustaceans, squid, young birds, insects, snails, fish, mollusks, and more. Gulls will even scavenge for garbage! Laughing gulls steal food from other birds, such as brown pelicans.

## A Common Sight

Herring gulls are the most easily recognized gulls of the North Atlantic. In fact, many people simply call them "seagulls," even though there are dozens of other species of gulls.

## Sibling Rivalry

The third herring gull chick to hatch will often weigh less, grow more slowly, and get less food than its siblings.

# Tough Jaws

A smiling barracuda is all sharp teeth and frightening fangs. If these teeth are worn or broken, new ones grow in to take their place. Not all barracudas are dangerous, but it never makes sense to trust one. Even if it's smiling.

**Barracudas come in a wide variety of sizes. The northern barracuda only grows to be 18 inches, while the great barracuda can grow to be 10 feet long!**

## Toxic

Don't eat the barracuda! People often become ill after eating the fish, because barracudas dine on reef fish that consume algae with a toxin in it.

## Fierce Chompers

Barracudas are known for their ferocious teeth. The lower jaw sticks out past the upper jaw, and both are filled with dozens of teeth. Some of these teeth point backwards to prevent fish from escaping from the great barracuda's mouth.

## SHINY!

Barracudas have a reputation for attacking humans while they swim, but they may not intentionally seek out humans. Barracudas hunt more by sight than by smell and are attracted to shiny objects. When a diver wears a watch or other jewelry into the water, the barracuda will see the reflection and come to investigate.

## FAST FOOD

Barracudas are speedy hunters. They can reach speeds of up to 36 miles per hour when attacking their prey. Sometimes barracudas follow sharks to eat leftover scraps from the sharks' meals.

# Unicorns, Blennies, and Bats, Oh My!

## Unicorn Horn

Only a few unicorn fish species have a bony hornlike structure on the forehead. This unique horn is not found on juveniles, but develops later in the fish's life.

## A-LURE-ING

The red-lipped batfish is a carnivore that eats small fish, mollusks, shrimp, and crabs. This deep-sea fish attracts its prey using a modified dorsal spine, similar to an anglerfish's lure.

Anglerfish

## RED-LIPPED BATFISH

The red-lipped batfish has evolved to have several odd adaptations. Its pectoral, pelvic, and anal fins are positioned on the body so that the batfish can rest on them while on the seafloor. It can move using its pectoral and pelvic fins as though it were walking!

## Pure Elegance

The elegant unicorn fish is found in the Indian Ocean. It is also known as the blonde naso tang, lipstick surgeonfish, and orangespine unicorn fish.

## Fangblenny

In the Indo-Pacific, there is a species of fangblenny that has a pair of recurved, or backwards-bent, fangs. These fangblennies use them for defense and territorial displays.

## Dirty Dealings

Several species of fangblenny will imitate the cleaner wrasse by hanging around the cleaning stations. Client fish will approach and then become victims of a sneak attack by the waiting fangblennies.

# Big, Friendly Sharks

Sharks are not always fierce and aggressive. Some sharks are harmless, and, strangely enough, the most harmless sharks are huge. These gentle giants include the basking shark, whale shark, and megamouth shark.

## LARGER THAN LIFE

The whale shark is the biggest fish in the world. Only about 100 have ever been seen. One captured near Pakistan in 1949 measured 41 feet long and was estimated to weigh 33,000 pounds.

# Sunbathers

A basking shark can grow to be 30 feet long and weigh 8,000 pounds. This fish is a mammoth sunbather. Its name comes from its habit of lying motionless in surface waters with its back above the surface and its nose and fins sticking out—as if it were basking in the sun.

## All Aboard

Believe it or not, whale sharks are so harmless, they let divers hold on to their fins for a ride. One diver has said the feeling is like clinging to an underwater freight train. When whale sharks become tired of their passengers, they dive deep into the sea.

## Mini Food

Plankton is the diet of these big sharks. Copepods—barely visible shrimplike creatures—are a large part of plankton. Scientists think that sharks eat about 1% of their bodyweight each day. For an 8,000-pound basking shark, that's a lot of plankton—80 pounds!

## THROAT STRAIN

These huge, plankton-eating sharks feed by keeping their mouths open while swimming forward. Whatever comes in is strained from the water by gill rakers at the backs of their throats. After awhile they swallow their catches. A cruising basking shark can strain about 2,000 gallons of water per hour.

# Diving Ducks

The female king eider is reddish-brown with black bars. This coloring provides camouflage, allowing her to blend in with her nest if she is threatened.

## YOUR HIGHNESS

The king eider is found in the Arctic Ocean, along the Arctic Circle. It gets its name because the male's head is brightly colored, resembling a crown.

## Feathered Friends

Spectacled eiders are unique from other eiders because their feathers extend all the way down to the nostrils on the bill. Both males and females share this feature. Like all other eider species, however, the male is much more colorful than the female.

## SPEC-TACULAR

Spectacled eiders certainly are a spectacular sight to see! Male spectacled eiders are colorful and have large white eye patches rimmed in black, which makes them appear to be wearing spectacles.

# SOLDIER ON

Steller's eider is the smallest and fastest of the four eider species. It is sometimes known as "soldier duck" because of its habit of swimming in flocks in single file.

## Flock Together

Common eiders gather in groups called crèches to help distract predators such as gulls from their ducklings. Crèches include mother eiders and other nonbreeding hens, along with anywhere from a few to over 150 ducklings.

## #1 Duck

The common eider is the largest of the eider species—in fact, it's the largest duck in the Northern Hemisphere! Common eiders are found mainly in the coastal Arctic regions of Siberia and Canada.

# Swords and Saws

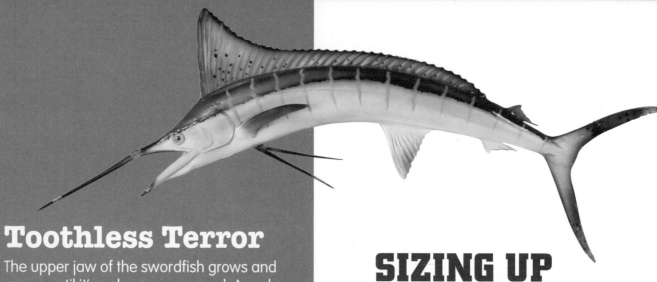

## Toothless Terror

The upper jaw of the swordfish grows and grows until it's a dangerous sword. A real slasher, the swordfish storms into a school of fish and rips its sword through whatever it can. Then, the eating begins—but not the chewing. The mighty swordfish, which can drive its sword through a wooden boat, has no teeth.

## SIZING UP

When a female spawns, she releases millions of buoyant eggs into the water for the male to fertilize. When they hatch, the larvae are only 4 millimeters long. An adult swordfish can grow to be more than 14 feet long.

## See Saw

It's easy to see how the sawfish, another member of the ray family, got its name. It has a sawlike snout with razor-sharp teeth on the outside. By simply thrashing its head from side to side through a school of fish, the sawfish gets plenty of food for dinner.

## Permanent Teeth

Sawfish never have to worry about losing their permanent teeth or having them wear out. Their teeth will grow throughout their whole lives.

## CENTRAL HEATING

Some fish can maintain a high body temperature that protects them from the cold ocean waters, but not the swordfish. Instead, it has a unique muscle and brown tissue that warms the blood flowing to its eyes and brain. This allows it to live in very cold ocean depths.

## SAWFISH

It's the perfect name for this member of the ray family. With a nose that could clear a forest, what else could it be called? Its sawlike snout, about one-third the fish's length, has 24 to 32 teeth. In a 20-foot sawfish, the saw can be 6 feet long!

# Salty Crocodiles

Saltwater crocodiles have a huge range. They can be found in the brackish and freshwater regions of Southeast Asia, eastern India, and northern Australia. They've also been seen swimming far out at sea.

## DOWN UNDER

Saltwater crocodiles can stay submerged underwater for more than an hour at a time. They have a valve in their throats that closes to keep them from drowning if they open their mouths underwater.

## Bite to Eat

Saltwater crocodiles will eat anything they can, including water buffalo, monkeys, and sharks! They'll explode from the water, grab their prey, and drag it back to the water to drown it before eating.

# Pair Matching

## Crocodile Conundrum

There are 5 crocodiles in each box, but only 3 matching pairs. Draw a line to connect 3 crocodiles in the top box to their identical twins in the box below.

# Fur Real

Fur seals and sea lions are in the family Otariidae, which comes from a Greek root word meaning "ear." Like sea lions, fur seals have external ears and thus are distinguished from what are considered to be true seals. They are also called eared seals.

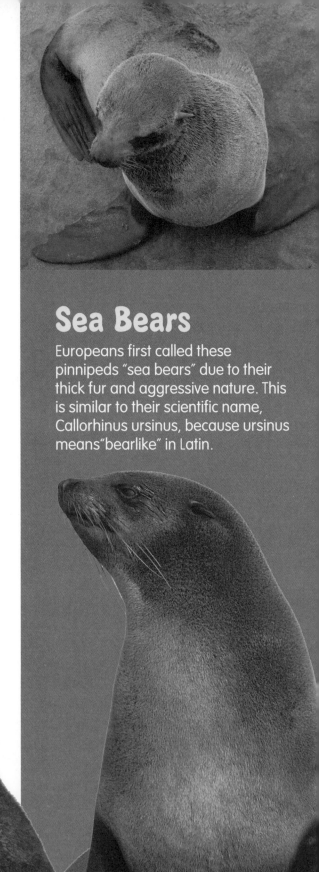

## Guys and Gals

Male fur seals, called bulls, can be three or more times the size of females! When it's time to breed, the bulls come ashore and stake out territory to claim as their own. Females, also known as cows, arrive later, and about five or more females will join each male.

## Sea Bears

Europeans first called these pinnipeds "sea bears" due to their thick fur and aggressive nature. This is similar to their scientific name, Callorhinus ursinus, because ursinus means "bearlike" in Latin.

## Land Legs

Fur seals move more easily on land than true seals do, because their back flippers can rotate and the front flippers extend to help move them forward. Their flippers are bare, with no fur covering them.

# Northern Fur Seal Cheat Sheet

- Northern fur seal cows return to sea to feed for a few days after nursing their pups for about a week. Once a breeding female returns to shore to nurse again, she recognizes her pup by its unique call and smell.

- The northern fur seal was nearly hunted to extinction in the 1800s. In 1911, these seals became protected by law. Since then, the population has increased to include over 1 million animals.

- These animals can sometimes be found "jughandling," keeping both front and back flippers outside the water while resting on the surface. Other eared seals and sea lions exhibit this behavior as well.

## DID YOU KNOW?

A large fur seal can gallop faster than a human can run!

# Maritime Bears

Polar bears are the only bears considered to be marine mammals, because they depend on the sea for their habitat and food. The Latin name for polar bear is *Ursus maritimus*, meaning "maritime bear," or a bear that lives on or near the sea.

## Mama Bear

Unlike other bear species, polar bears do not hibernate in the winter. However, pregnant females make dens in earth and deep snowbanks, where they stay throughout winter and give birth to one to three cubs. The mothers come out of the dens with their young in the spring, when they teach the cubs how to hunt.

## CHILL OUT

It's freezing up there near the North Pole! Luckily, these furry creatures are well-adapted to the cold, snowy environment. Polar bears have special features that help them stay warm, including fur on the bottom of their paws, layers of fat called blubber underneath their thick fur, and black skin that absorbs sunlight.

NORTH POLE

## KING SIZE

Polar bears are generally considered to be the largest bear species on Earth. Adults are usually between 7¼ and 8 feet tall when standing, but male polar bears can grow up to 10 feet and weigh over 1,500 pounds!

## What's for Dinner?

Seals are a polar bear's favorite meal. Though polar bears are skilled swimmers, they aren't fast enough to catch seals in open water. Instead, they wait on the ice near cracks and seal breathing holes and snatch seals as they come to the surface!

## Bear Solitaire

Polar bears are found in the Arctic, in Canada, Denmark, Russia, Norway, and Alaska in the United States. These bears have no natural predators in the wild and are often a solitary species.

## WELL-DRESSED

Polar bears look white, but their fur is clear with a hollow core, or inside. The fur reflects sunlight, making the bears appear white and allowing them to blend in with the snow—a trick that comes in handy when hunting seals! The fur is water-repellent, allowing the polar bears to easily shake off water.

167

# Barnacles

Barnacles are crustaceans. Scientists used to think that they were related to snails, but they are actually more closely related to crabs!

## Acorns Aplenty

There are over 1,400 species of barnacles in the world. The most common barnacle is the acorn barnacle.

## Tall Tale

The goose barnacle has a fascinating story! The goose barnacle is said to resemble the head and neck of a species of goose called the barnacle goose. Since people in Britain had never seen a nest or egg of a barnacle goose, they said that the geese were born from the goose barnacle, emerging fully feathered. Since people believed the goose was born from a barnacle, they decided it could be eaten on Fridays and throughout Lent, contrary to what the Catholic Church said!

## In Place

Goose barnacles are hermaphrodites. This allows them to release their eggs into larvae, which drift with the tides until they attach themselves to an object. Once they have attached themselves, they will not move again unless torn off.

## Feeding Feet

Barnacles are sessile, meaning they are fixed in one place, so they don't need to use their legs to walk. They've adapted their legs for a different purpose over the years. Now, barnacle legs, called cirri, sweep tiny particles of food from the water into the barnacle's mouth.

### STUCK ON YOU

Barnacles will attach themselves to the hulls of ships, which can cause the ships to drag in the water. When the ships dock, the barnacles are removed. In some countries, they are sold as food.

# Oarfish and Wahoos

## SIGHT UNSEEN

Giant oarfish are rarely seen, because, scientists believe, they live as deep as 3,300 feet below the surface. They can weigh up to 600 pounds.

A wahoo is bluish-green on the upper part of its body and fades to silver on the bottom. Each wahoo has 25 to 30 stripes.

## WAHOO!

Wahoos, also called onos, can be found in tropical and subtropical oceans all over the world. They are closely related to the mackerel.

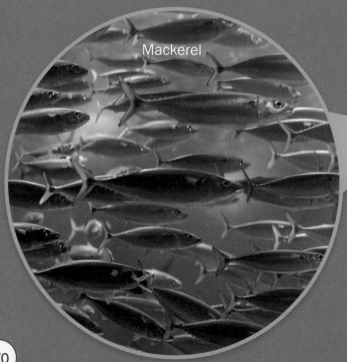

Mackerel

170

## FISH FOLKLORE

Oarfish feature in historic tales and folklore about sea serpents and sea monsters. However, these fish are harmless to people—they have flimsy gill rakers, instead of teeth, to help them catch plankton."

## Godsent

In Japan, the slender oarfish is known as the "Messenger from the Sea God's Palace," and the sight of many slender oarfish washing up on shore is traditionally believed to signal an oncoming earthquake. Scientists think that oarfish are more sensitive to the movements of fault lines in the earth because they live so close to the bottom of the ocean.

## Tear It Up

Wahoos can travel at very high speeds, which helps them catch other fish and squids. Their sharp, serrated teeth help them to tear larger prey into smaller, bite-sized pieces.

# Shark Sense

## Good Vibrations

A shark can hear movement in the water, but it can also feel the vibrations by using its lateral line, a line of canals running from head to tail that is linked to the surface of the shark. Each canal contains special sensory cells with hairlike projections that move with vibrations in the water and send messages to the shark's brain.

## Night Sight

What do cats and sharks have in common? Their eyes. Both have eyes with a mirrorlike layer that reflects light. This physical trait allows them to see better in the dark. So, whether in clear water or murky seas, a shark can still hunt.

## BLINK

Most fish have no eyelids, but some sharks have three—an upper, a lower, and a second lower lid. This second lower lid, called a nictitating membrane, can clamp shut and protect the whole eye in dangerous situations.

## SUPERSHARP SENSES

A shark can hear, smell, and feel everything in the water—at great distances. With these supersharp senses, the shark has an excellent design for hunting. A school of fish may be passing through, or a fish may be hurt. The shark knows the difference and it reacts quickly, zooming toward its prey with deadly accuracy.

## Smart Shark

Sharks are often thought of as "swimming noses"—that they only use their brains to smell out food. Some, however, are fairly smart and can learn. Generally, the more active, fast-moving sharks have brains that are more complex than those of slower, bottom-dwelling sharks.

## SWIMMING NOSE

Two-thirds of a shark's brain controls its sense of smell. The two nostrils on a shark's snout are full of cells that detect odors in the water. In one experiment, sharks smelled a small bit of tuna from 75 feet away—smelling one-part tuna juice to 1½ million parts water.

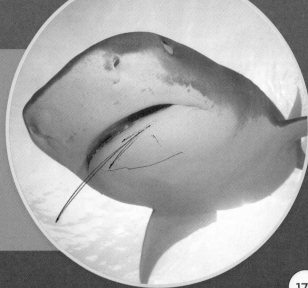

# Abalone

Abalone are sea snails. They may look like clams, but they only have one shell. The underside of the shell contains its foot muscle, which it uses to move. The foot is very strong—it has suction power equal to 4,000 times its weight.

## What a Gem

The abalone shell is used for decoration. The inside has a beautiful layer of mother-of-pearl, which is used in jewelry, buttons, buckles, and inlay.

## Preyed Upon

Blacklip abalone eat seagrass leaves and red algae. They have many predators, including crabs, sea stars, stingrays, wobbegong sharks, otters, and humans.

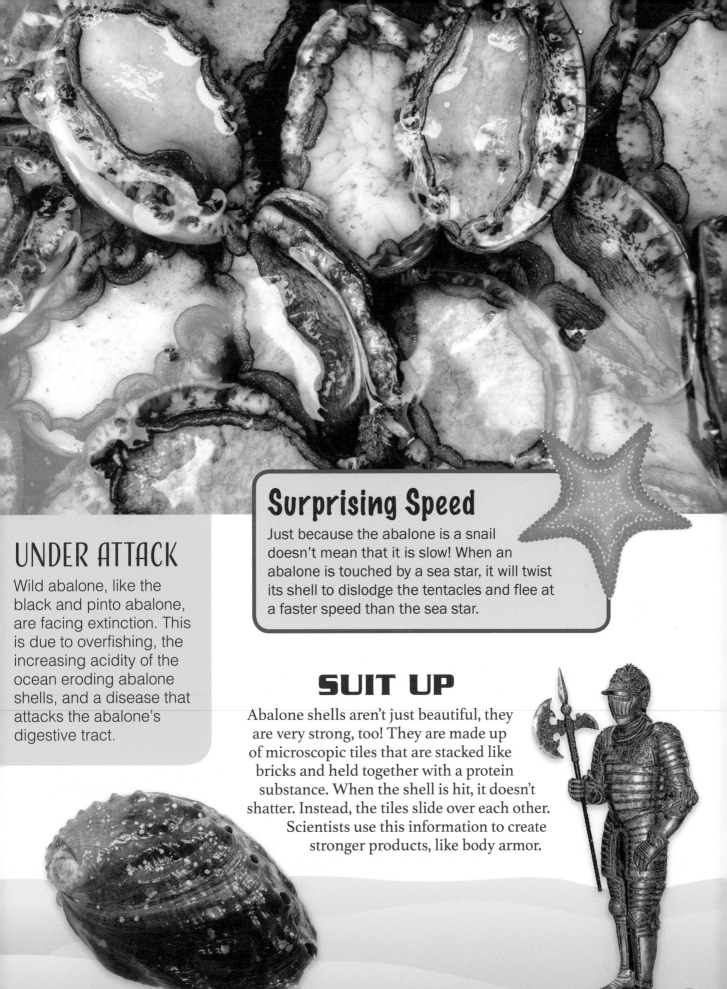

## Surprising Speed

Just because the abalone is a snail doesn't mean that it is slow! When an abalone is touched by a sea star, it will twist its shell to dislodge the tentacles and flee at a faster speed than the sea star.

## UNDER ATTACK

Wild abalone, like the black and pinto abalone, are facing extinction. This is due to overfishing, the increasing acidity of the ocean eroding abalone shells, and a disease that attacks the abalone's digestive tract.

## SUIT UP

Abalone shells aren't just beautiful, they are very strong, too! They are made up of microscopic tiles that are stacked like bricks and held together with a protein substance. When the shell is hit, it doesn't shatter. Instead, the tiles slide over each other. Scientists use this information to create stronger products, like body armor.

# Shark-filled Waters

## World Travelers

Sharks live all over the ocean, in cold to temperate waters—usually cooler than 90°F. Some live in shallow waters, while others live in the deep and on the ocean floor. The bull shark can even swim from salt water into freshwater. Bull sharks have been found in the Mississippi River.

## BRUTAL BULL

The bull shark doesn't look as frightening as the great white, but it is in some ways more dangerous—certainly in the tropics. Listed as the third-most dangerous man-eater, the bull shark swims in places that people do—in salt water and freshwater.

## BULL-HEADED

Bull sharks get their name from the look of their short, blunt snouts and their tendency to head-butt their prey before attacking.

## Warm Weather

Blacktip sharks can be found in warm coastal waters around the world and in bays, estuaries, coral reefs, and shallow waters near beaches and river mouths. This means that they are often encountered by humans, and their habitats are easily threatened by fishing and coastal development.

## A Big Threat

The blacktip shark is considered near threatened by conservation agencies. This is due to the destruction of their habitats and because they are considered a tasty meal. Their fins are often cut off and used in shark fin soup.

## LEAPS AND BOUNDS

Blacktip sharks can sometimes be seen leaping from the water, rotating several times, and splashing down on their backs. This is part of a hunting method in which the sharks hurl themselves at schools of fish near the surface of the water.

# Bright Scales

## Just Dotty

There are about 100 different species of dottybacks. They are mostly very colorful fish, although there are differences in color between males and females, which is referred to as sexual dimorphism.

## Here Be Dragonets

Most of the 400 dragonet species are bottom-dwellers and can be found burying themselves in the sand at the bottom of shallow waters. Only a few species live in deep waters.

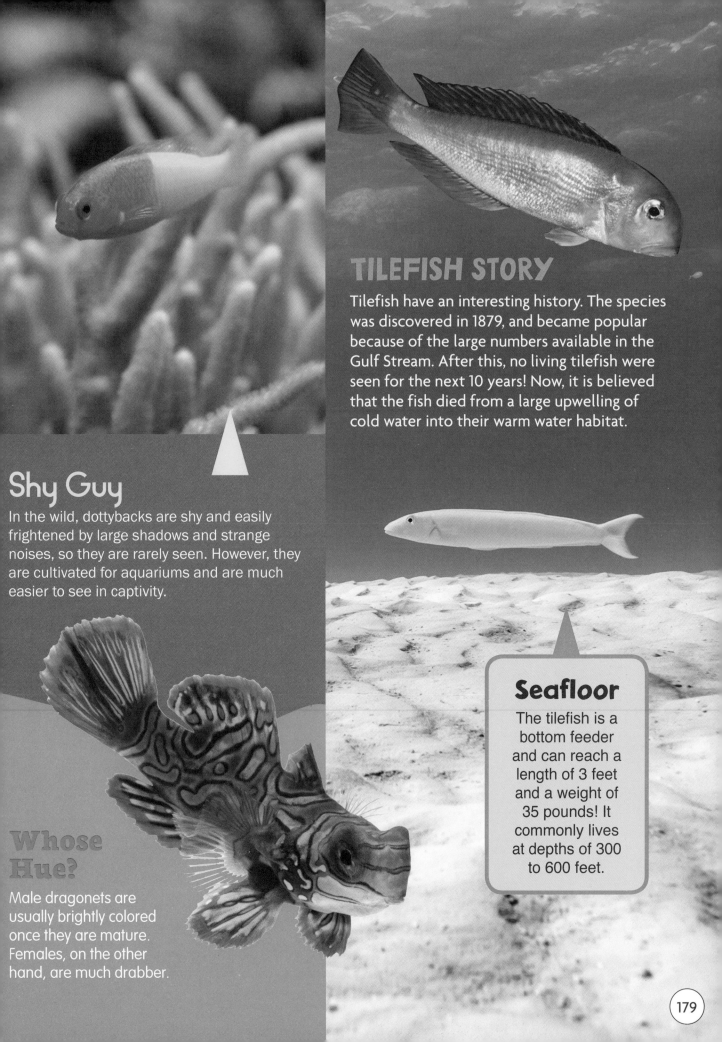

## TILEFISH STORY

Tilefish have an interesting history. The species was discovered in 1879, and became popular because of the large numbers available in the Gulf Stream. After this, no living tilefish were seen for the next 10 years! Now, it is believed that the fish died from a large upwelling of cold water into their warm water habitat.

## Shy Guy

In the wild, dottybacks are shy and easily frightened by large shadows and strange noises, so they are rarely seen. However, they are cultivated for aquariums and are much easier to see in captivity.

### Seafloor

The tilefish is a bottom feeder and can reach a length of 3 feet and a weight of 35 pounds! It commonly lives at depths of 300 to 600 feet.

## Whose Hue?

Male dragonets are usually brightly colored once they are mature. Females, on the other hand, are much drabber.

# Zebra Turkey Fish

The zebra turkey fish, also called the zebra lionfish, is native to shallow reefs in the Indo-Pacific region. Because aquarium owners have released zebra turkey fish into the wild, these fish have been spotted in the Atlantic as far north as New York.

## Safety in Spines

Despite its fearsome appearance and poisonous spines, the zebra turkey fish only eats small, bottom-dwelling crustaceans. Its only natural enemy is the grouper, probably because the other fish aren't willing to take a chance on those poisonous spines!

## Striped Beauty

This beautiful, elegant fish grows up to 12 inches long. It has stripes that range in color from red and brown to black and white. It has 13 poison-filled spines on its dorsal fin, but these are only used for defense.

# Word Scramble

## Under the Sea

Unscramble the letters to find the names of some fascinating water-dwelling animals.

**HILNIFSO**

— — — — — — — —

**ROUGPER**

— — — — — — —

**LEBU EWLAH**

— — — — — — — — —

**KHELW**

— — — — —

**TABTE ISFH**

— — — — — — — — —

**GRERHNI**

— — — — — — —

**TRAGE EHWIT KAHSR**

— — — — — — — — — — — — — —

**NOMO FELISLYJH**

— — — — — — — — — — — —

**NIGAT DUSIQ**

— — — — — — — — — —

**ACDNIRAL HSFI**

— — — — — — — — — — —

# Well-known Fish

## Herring Hordes

Silversides, as herring fry are called, hatch from sticky eggs that cling to stones, sand, and seaweed. Adult females, traveling in gigantic schools, lay their eggs at the same time, around 30,000 each. That's why there are so many herring in the world—they are one of the most numerous of all vertebrates.

## FISH FAMILY

Herring is the common name for members of the family Clupeidae, which includes many species of marine and freshwater fish, such as sardines, menhaden, and shad. Herring swim in gigantic schools and feed on plankton, small animals, and plants.

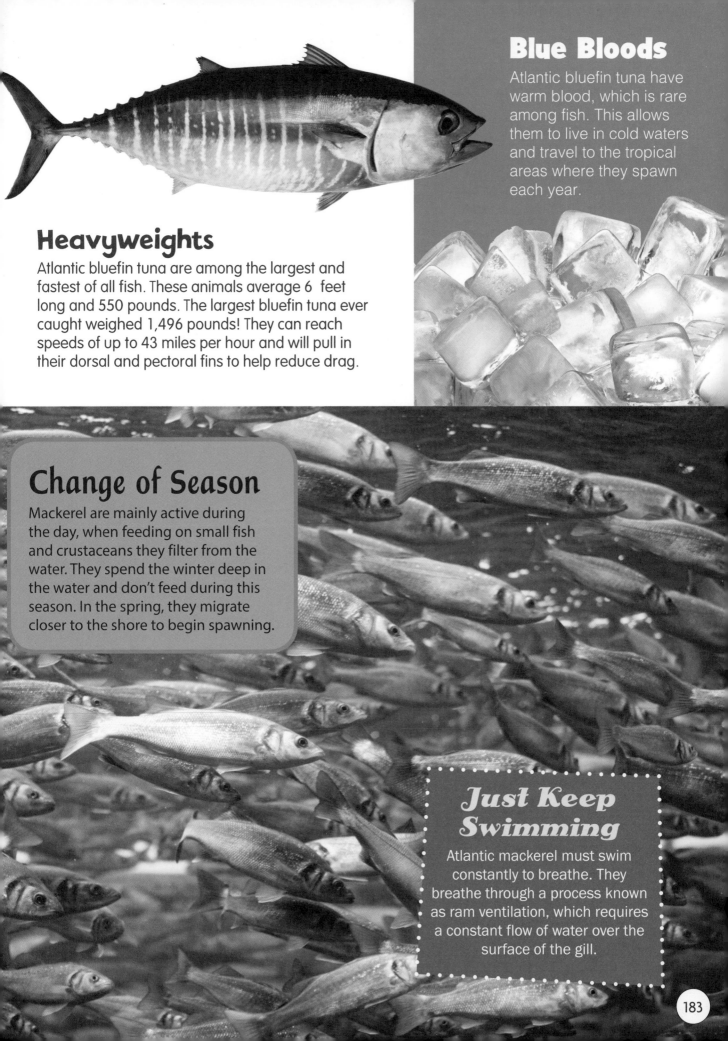

## Blue Bloods

Atlantic bluefin tuna have warm blood, which is rare among fish. This allows them to live in cold waters and travel to the tropical areas where they spawn each year.

## Heavyweights

Atlantic bluefin tuna are among the largest and fastest of all fish. These animals average 6 feet long and 550 pounds. The largest bluefin tuna ever caught weighed 1,496 pounds! They can reach speeds of up to 43 miles per hour and will pull in their dorsal and pectoral fins to help reduce drag.

## Change of Season

Mackerel are mainly active during the day, when feeding on small fish and crustaceans they filter from the water. They spend the winter deep in the water and don't feed during this season. In the spring, they migrate closer to the shore to begin spawning.

## Just Keep Swimming

Atlantic mackerel must swim constantly to breathe. They breathe through a process known as ram ventilation, which requires a constant flow of water over the surface of the gill.

# Whales, Dolphins, and People

Because of their size and speed, whales have few natural enemies besides humans. In the 19th century, people hunted whales to near extinction for oil, baleen, and meat. Baleen was used like plastic is today, in products like brushes and corsets. A few nations still practice whaling, but most have now stopped.

## NYLON NICKS

Even nylon fishing lines that float on the sea can severely injure dolphins and whales. The animal gets entangled, and the line cuts through its flesh, sometimes cutting off the dorsal fin.

## Net Loss

Many dolphins and porpoises get trapped in fishing nets. Unable to surface and breathe air, the water mammals drown. Drift nets, some big enough to encircle the city of New York, are set for fish but catch everything. Because the fishermen want only the fish, they simply throw the bodies of the dead dolphins and porpoises back overboard.

## Mammal Get-together

Whale-watching groups go out to sea in hopes of meeting whales. Getting close to these magnificent mammals is an exciting experience.

## Toxic Waters

Pollution is the greatest threat whales face today. Oil spills, toxic waste, and sewage dumping affect the foods that whales eat and become toxins in their systems. Some scientists believe that pollution harms the whales' navigating systems, causing some to swim into shallow waters and wash ashore.

## Friendly Folks

Many people and organizations are now working to secure a safer future for dolphins and whales.

# Auks

An auk is any of the 22 species—21 living—of diving birds in the family Alcidae, including the great auk, little auk, and razorbill. Auks completely depend on the ocean for food, since their diet is made up of fish, crustaceans, mollusks, and plankton.

## The Greatest

The great auk has been extinct since June 3, 1844, when the last two were killed in Iceland. These birds were hunted for their meat and feathers. They were easy to kill, since they were flightless, and they couldn't breed fast enough to replace the killed birds.

## Misnomer

It is widely agreed that the word "penguin" was once used as the name for the great auk. Centuries ago, sailors may have mistaken penguins for great auks.

## Buoy-ing!

The little auk captures its food by diving up to 115 feet under the water and letting its natural buoyancy help it swim upwards in a zig-zag motion before capturing its prey. The little auk will sometimes feed at night, when its prey of tiny marine crustaceans comes closer to the surface of the water.

## No Neck

The little auk, as its name suggests, is the smallest of the auks. It is only about 6 inches long, and its body is so short and fat that it appears to have no neck.

## CALL ME

The razorbill is called a "murre" in Cornwall, probably based on the sound of its call. Its genus name, *Alca*, may derive from the Icelandic name for the bird, *Alka*, which may be an imitation of another razorbill call: "arcc-arcc."

## Unique Beak

The razor-billed auk, or razorbill, can be recognized by its deep, wedge-shaped bill that is flattened on the end and has a white line. While the species isn't normally very vocal, these birds often produce a deep, croaking "urrr" sound when they breed.

# Strange and Scary

## CRUNCH!

The cookiecutter shark is a 20-inch long creature that feeds on whales and dolphins. With its circular set of teeth, the cookiecutter chomps a perfectly round hole out of its victim. Its teeth are so sharp, it has damaged rubber-covered parts of submarines.

## Toothy Grin

The cookiecutter shark has 30 to 37 small teeth in its upper jaw and 25 to 31 larger triangular teeth in its lower jaw. The teeth are connected at their bases, allowing the shark to move the entire row of teeth if one is touched. This also means that the teeth are lost as a whole unit instead of individually. Cookiecutter sharks swallow their lost teeth, a behavior that is thought to help maintain the levels of calcium in the sharks' bodies.

## Old-fashioned

Cow sharks are considered to be the most primitive of all living sharks. This is because they have a skeleton like those found in extinct shark fossils, a relatively primitive digestive system, and six to seven pairs of gill slits rather than five like most modern sharks.

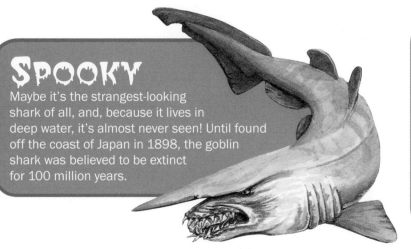

## SPOOKY

Maybe it's the strangest-looking shark of all, and, because it lives in deep water, it's almost never seen! Until found off the coast of Japan in 1898, the goblin shark was believed to be extinct for 100 million years.

## Open Wide!

A goblin shark can extend its jaw out of its mouth to catch prey. When it sees a fish or squid just out of reach, the goblin shark will stretch the 3-inch elastic tissue attached to its upper and lower jaws and thrust out its teeth to grab it!

# Sea Unicorns

Those long, spiraled tusks breaking the surface of the Arctic Ocean do not belong to a herd of mythical creatures. Attached to these tusks are fantastical-looking animals—often dubbed "unicorns of the sea"—called narwhals, a species of whales. A narwhal's "horn" is in fact a long tooth.

## Social Butterflies

Narwhals are very social! They commonly travel in groups, called pods, of around 15 to 20 individuals, but they may gather in groups of up to 100 or more.

## HEAD TURNERS

Narwhals are closely related to beluga whales. Both species have very flexible necks, so they can easily turn their heads in the water.

## Tusk Tasks

Scientists are not quite sure why narwhals have tusks. One possible explanation is that the tusks are used to impress females or to fight rival males, but they may serve other purposes as well. The tusks are covered in nerves and tiny holes that let water in, which may allow them to detect temperature change or a shift in the water's saltiness.

## Breathing Room

Like other marine mammals, narwhals cannot breathe underwater and must breach, or come up for air. While they like to stay near the surface, they are capable of diving close to 5,000 feet deep!

## DID YOU KNOW?

Narwhals change color as they age. These beautiful animals are blue-gray when they are born and darken to a blue-black shade as juveniles. Adults are a mottled, or blotchy, gray, and their skin gets lighter as they grow older.

# Atlantic Fish

Both the Atlantic wolffish and the Atlantic giant grouper are naturally rare due to their place at the top of the food chain and their slow maturation, but they play very important roles in the health of their habitats. The Atlantic wolffish helps regulate the number of sea urchins and other invertebrates, and the Atlantic giant grouper helps keep the reefs where it lives healthy.

## DEEP BLUE SEA

The Atlantic wolffish can be found deep in the cold waters of the Atlantic Ocean, mainly from Maine to Iceland to the British Isles. The wolffish has several compounds in its blood that prevent it from freezing.

## Weird Wolf

With its large head, big mouth, and long body, the wolffish can look very weird. It has a lot of sharp teeth, and its bite can cause serious harm. Its strong jaws and teeth can bite off fingers, and can even chomp through steel and wood! Those powerful teeth are used to crush the wolffish's favorite foods, such as sea stars, crabs, and sea urchins.

## Ambush Attack

The Atlantic goliath grouper, like most groupers, is an ambush predator, which means that it lies in wait for its prey to come along and attacks it instead of actively hunting. It eats large fish, invertebrates, and even some small sharks. These groupers do not chew! Instead, they use their giant mouths to create a vacuum that sucks in their prey so they can swallow them whole!

## GIANT GROUPER

There's a reason the Atlantic goliath grouper shares its name with a biblical giant: This fish can reach lengths of 8 feet and weigh up to 700 pounds. It is one of the largest groupers in the world!

## GROUPER GROUPS

During the year, these groupers are not seen in large numbers in a single area, but this changes during reproduction. Between June and December, right after the full moons, the fish can gather in groups of at least 100, called spawning aggregations.

# Search & Find®
## Tropical Fish

Search & Find®
these 7 different
tropical fish in the
coral reef below.

# Black, White, and Red

## Big Bird

The Laysan albatross is a very large bird with an impressive wingspan. The body of the bird can be 2.6 feet long and its wings can reach a span of 6.9 feet! Males of this species are slightly larger than the females.

## Mates for Life

Laysan albatrosses reach maturity at eight to nine years, at which time they switch from permanently living at sea to living on land for 10 months per year. During their months on land, albatross mates will raise a single chick. Breeding pairs will mate for life, which is nearly 40 years!

# Ready for Takeoff

Red-footed boobies can easily fly long distances, but taking off is tricky! These birds need wind for a graceful takeoff—without it, they can be seen half-running, half-flying in an attempt to gather enough momentum to get off the ground. When the red-footed booby is in the water, it will thrust its feet back simultaneously and jump forward into the wind to lift off into the air.

## LOOK UP

The red-footed booby is mainly pelagic, only coming to shore to breed. During breeding, male red-footed boobies attract a mate by "sky-pointing," a practice where they point their beaks directly upwards.

## EATING HABITS

The red-legged cormorant mainly eats fish and invertebrates and will hunt alone or in a flock. When pursuing prey, red-legged cormorants can dive to depths of about 49 feet and forage along the seabed.

## Shuffle Along

When a red-legged cormorant is on land, it is less agile than it is in the water. It doesn't like to shuffle more than a few steps at a time and prefers to fly from one area to another.

## REPURPOSED MATERIAL

Red-legged cormorants typically build their nests on narrow ledges in steep cliffs, high up in sea caves, or on small, rocky islets. Their nests are made of seaweed, feathers, guano, and sometimes items like plastic bags.

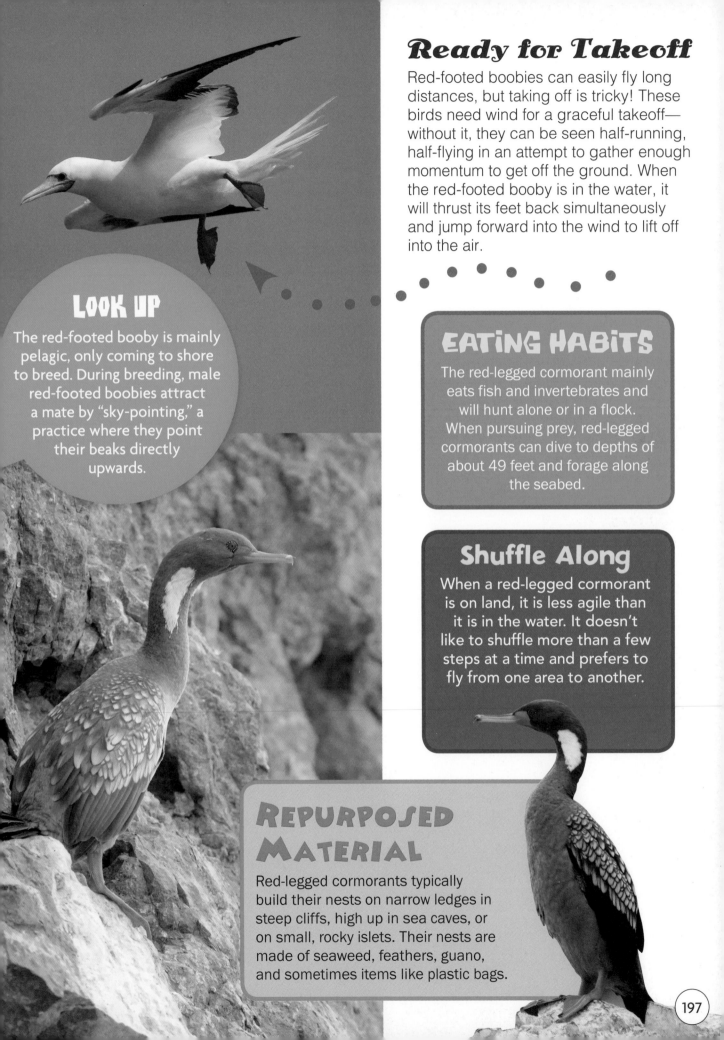

197

# Seal Sighting

## Familiar Faces

The Weddell seal is the most southerly breeding mammal in the world and one of the best-known seal species in the Antarctic. The male and female Weddell seals have similar appearances, but the female may be slightly larger.

## Hold Your Breath

The Weddell seal is a great diver. It can reach depths of nearly 1,968½ feet and swim 3.1 miles on a single breath. It can spend up to 82 minutes underwater before it needs to surface to breathe.

## Ring Tones

Weddell seals have at least 34 different call types on record, making them one of the noisiest seal species! Their calls involve whistles, buzzes, tweets, and chirps that vary from region to region and can be heard for some distance—even through the ice!

# HiDDEN LAiRS

Female ringed seals build lairs on fast ice, or ice along coasts, to give birth. These lairs serve a couple of purposes, but mainly they are used for protection from predators and from the frigid temperatures. A ringed seal has several lairs among which she will move her pup to avoid predators. Soon after birth, the pup can move among the lairs by itself.

## Primary Predators

The ringed seal's main predator is the polar bear, but the seals are also threatened by walruses, killer whales, Arctic foxes, gulls, and ravens. The ringed seal eats mainly small fish but will eat crustaceans like krill and shrimp when they are readily available.

## SMALL SEAL

The ringed seal is the smallest living seal species, growing up to only about 5 feet in length. It gets its name from the ring-shaped marks on its fur, and its face has been said to resemble that of a cat.

# Stargazers and Wreckfish

## Stargazing

There are four types of stargazers: northern, southern, speckled, and masked. These fish have been found all over the world in both tropical and temperate waters and can be identified by the eyes and mouth on top of the head, instead of where they're normally located.

# DANGER!

Stargazers have a couple of adaptations to ward off predators: Modified eye muscles allow them to deliver shocks of up to 50 volts to fish that get close enough to investigate, and poisonous spines encourage predatory fish to stay away.

# I'm Waiting

A stargazer buries itself in the sand, leaving only its eyes uncovered, lying in wait for its prey. Some species of stargazers have a lure protruding from their mouths to help attract prey.

# Life Stages

Wreckfish have two distinct life stages: The first, the juvenile stage, lasts for more than two years. During this time, the wreckfish lives nearer to the surface in the open ocean and feeds on bony fish. For the second stage, it settles on the bottom of the ocean where it continues to eat fish and occasionally squids.

# LONG-LIVED

The wreckfish is a large fish that can reach a maximum length of about 7 feet and a weight of 220 pounds. These fish can live for a long time. In fact, the oldest recorded male was found to be 81 years old, and the oldest female was 64 years old!

# Ground Sharks

## Smooth Operator

The silky shark has beautiful, smooth, almost metallic skin, but don't be deceived by its appealing appearance—this shark is a very active hunter with extremely good hearing!

## Degrees of Danger

The silky shark is classified as near threatened because it is a popular catch for the shark leather trade. It is also fished for its fins, meat, and liver oil. It is considered the third most popular fish for the fin trade, with an estimated 1½ million fins traded every year. Scientists aren't sure how many silky sharks there are in the wild, making it difficult to tell exactly how endangered the sea animals are.

## Pin Head

The hammerhead shark's head is specifically adapted to help it catch its favorite food: stingrays. It uses its wide head to pin the stingray to the ocean floor before eating it. If the shark can't find a stingray, it will also eat bony fish, crabs, squids, lobsters, and other creatures.

A great hammerhead is sometimes found in water only **3 feet deep.**

# Sweet William

The gummy shark gets its name from the shape of its teeth, which are flat and arranged in a pattern like snake scales. This makes them perfect for crushing food instead of tearing it. Another name for the gummy shark is the Sweet William. This was given to the species as a joke, since the shark's flesh smells terrible.

# Hammer Horror

Seeing a hammerhead in the water might be enough to scare a swimmer to death, but scientists don't think that hammerheads are man-eaters. However, they consider a few kinds, like the great hammerhead and the smooth hammerhead, to be potentially dangerous because of their size.

# Gummy Vitamins

Gummy sharks can be found in Australia, and are sometimes sold as "flake" in fish 'n 'chips. Gummy shark liver contains a high level of vitamin A, which led to overfishing until the end of World War II and the discovery of artificial vitamin A. Now, gummy sharks are protected, with limits on the amount that fishermen can catch, and Australia encourages the use of other, more sustainable fish for a delicious basket of fish 'n' chips.

# Humpback Whales

Look! It's a giant humpback whale swimming in the ocean! People come from all over the world to try to get a glimpse of these whales breaching. Humpbacks are also known for their "songs"—musical sounds that travel through the water. Scientists study the moaning, crying, and howling noises to try to find out what they mean.

## Mommy and Baby

Mother humpback whales swim close to their young. They often touch each other with their flippers—just like a mother and child holding hands. The baby humpback whale might grow as long as 60 feet as an adult and weigh as much as 40 tons.

# Hungry Herd

Group living is safer when enemies like sharks and killer whales are nearby. It also makes it easier for some whales to catch and find food. Species like the humpback whale sometimes gather in large groups and drive fish into a concentrated area. This is called cooperative feeding.

## It's a Fluke

Humpback whales raise their flukes when diving. Humpback fluke patterns are like fingerprints. Scientist use them to tell individual whales apart.

# Marine Snails

## Deceiving Looks

Moon snails may look like pretty, innocent shelled creatures, but they are quite ferocious predators. A moon snail will use its radula, a group of seven rows of teeth, to make a hole in a clam to open its shell and eat the meat inside.

## Sacred Shells

Cowries are marine snails with glossy, egg-shaped shells. Cowrie shells have been highly valued over the years, used throughout the South Pacific as money and religious symbols.

## DID YOU KNOW?

The moon snail can expand its body to be much larger than its shell when it is fully extended. It does this by inflating its tissues with seawater.

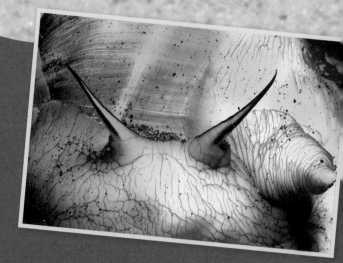

# Seashells Spotted

If you've ever visited a beach along the Atlantic Coast or the Gulf Coast, chances are that you've seen whelk shells on the sand. Whelks are sea snails with spiral shells and a muscular foot. They vary in size from around 1 inch to over 1 foot long!

**THE SHY COWRIES ARE NOCTURNAL, MEANING THEY ARE MOST ACTIVE AT NIGHT. DURING THE DAY, THEY HIDE THEMSELVES AMONG ROCKS AND CORAL IN TROPICAL WATERS.**

# Tame Tigers

Tiger cowries are herbivores, meaning they only eat plants. Their meal of choice includes seaweed and algae.

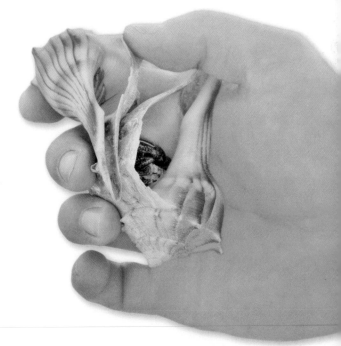

# Lightning Strikes

The lightning whelk is the official state shell of Texas. These snails are named for the lightning-like zig-zag pattern of brown markings on juvenile lightning whelks.

# Winging It

## MIGHTY WINGS

The southern giant petrel has a wingspan of 3½ to 6.7 feet and weighs about 11 pounds. This bird can be mistaken for an albatross, but it has a larger bill, narrower and shorter wings, and a humpbacked appearance.

## On the Hunt

When blue-footed boobies hunt for fish, they dive beneath the water in two ways: Either they zip through the water, floating just below the surface, or they dive from heights of up to 80 feet in the air. Once they spot a school of fish, the booby will fold back its wings, break into the water like a bullet, and grab fish with its long beak.

## Blue Shoes

The male blue-footed booby shows off during mating season by dramatically strutting around to show off his feet. The female normally chooses the male with the bluest feet as a mating partner.

# Scavengers

Southern giant petrels are mainly scavengers, which means that they eat dead animals, plants, or garbage. They mainly eat seal and penguin carcasses, offal, garbage from ships, and discarded fish. However, they will also attack penguins and other birds, krill and other crustaceans, fish, and squid.

# Live and Prosper

Scientists think that the northern fulmar is one of the longest-living bird species. A northern fulmar can live an average of 32 years. Some northern fulmars in Scotland were banded in 1951 as adults and were found still breeding in 1990, meaning they were likely more than 50 years old!

# Slick Trick

Fulmars have a special stomach oil that they store in a gland called the proventriculus. This oil serves two purposes: A fulmar can use the oil for defense, spraying it onto an approaching predatory bird and gumming up the attacker's wings so that the predator falls out of the sky. The second use is for energy. Fulmars can regurgitate this oil to use as fuel on long flights or to feed their young.

# Pretty Deadly

The Indian Ocean is home to some magnificent but dangerous creatures, such as the venomous mauve stinger. The mauve stinger's scientific name is *Pelagia noctiluca*, which roughly translates to "night light" (*noctiluca*) "of the sea" (*Pelagia*), because of its ability to produce light. Its sting is not deadly to humans, but it often will cause scars.

## Warning Sign

Striped surgeonfish found in the Indo-Pacific reefs are easily recognized by their vibrant blue and yellow stripes. These attractive animals come equipped with venom in their caudal, or tail, spine.

## Toxic Beauty

Mandarinfish, otherwise known as mandarin dragonets, are arguably the most beautiful fish in the sea, but there is more to them than meets the eye. These colorful fish are covered in tiny spines that will inject a toxic mucus into predators that try to eat them.

## BEAUTIFUL DANGER

Cone snail shells are popularly used in decorations and jewelry, but you wouldn't want to touch a live member of this genus. There are hundreds of species of cone snails, and all of them possess a sting to capture and paralyze prey. A few cone snail species, such as the textile cone, have venom powerful enough to severely harm and even kill humans.

## DID YOU KNOW?

Scientists study the venom in sea creatures to see how its components can be used in medicine. Some toxins from cone snails, called conantoxins, have been tested for use against epileptic seizures.

# Crack the Code

## Secrets of the Sea

Use the key below to crack the code and find out which sea creatures produce venom that is being studied or used to create medication for humans.

A=1  C=2  E=3  I=4  L=5  M=6  N=7  O=8  S=9

S E A
9 3 1

A N E M O N E
1 7 3 6 8 7 3

C O N E
2 8 7 3

S N A I L
9 7 1 4 5

# Sharks and People

The shark is often used as a symbol for things that are frightening or dangerous, but scientists have studied sharks enough not to think of them simply as killing machines. In fact, people are more dangerous to sharks than sharks are to people. We hunt them, pollute their water, and cause them injury, sometimes depleting whole populations.

## Domino Effect

Sharks are considered keystone species—that is, they have an essential role as top predators in balancing other populations in their ecosystems. Without sharks, larger fish populations grow and feed on herbivores, which reduces the number of herbivores that can consume algae. Coral reefs are unable to compete with the increased amount of algae, and suffer as a result. Healthy ocean ecosystems rely on healthy shark populations!

## The Danger Zone

There are 20 different species of sharks listed as endangered or threatened species, but conservation efforts like research, working with local fishermen, and restricting harvests have helped reduce overfishing and are making a path for sustainable shark species development.

# STUDY BUDDY

Scientists study sharks to find out more about them, but it's not easy. When you can locate them in the vast open sea, they're not always doing the things that you want to find out about, such as giving birth, schooling, or sleeping. Scientists have come up with procedures, like tagging and tracking, to get to know sharks better.

## HELP PROTECT SHARKS!

## Aquatic Advocate

If you want to do something today to help protect sharks, one thing you can do is tell people—like your friends, classmates, and teachers—about how important sharks are, and how often they are misrepresented. If we can replace the negative stereotypes surrounding sharks with real information, we can better protect these essential predators!

# TREASURED TEETH

Shark teeth have been treasured for hundreds of years. People used to use fossilized teeth as charms to ward off evil and protect against poisoning. Pacific Islanders used shark teeth to make weapons. Today, people make jewelry out of shark teeth.

# Family Ties

A baby whale, called a calf, is extremely close to its mother. From the moment of its underwater birth, a calf is totally dependent on her. The two will spend many months together, sometimes years, before the young calf can take of itself.

## Baby Love

Because calves are very playful, they sometimes get into trouble. Often aunts will help take care of them, but mothers still watch their babies closely. When a calf disobeys, its mother butts it with her head. She also protects her baby by using her flippers to hold it close to her body.

## Free Ride

Calves follow closely at their mothers' sides. Some keep up by riding their mothers' waves and underwater currents. The flow of water over the mothers' bodies helps pull the calves along. For a really easy ride, babies will hang on to their mothers' fins.

## Copy-cat Calf

Calves learn by imitating. They turn, dive, and surface right along with their mothers. But whale mothers aren't just teachers. They're also playmates. Gray whale mothers play a special game with their babies. They swim underneath them and blow bubbles out their blowholes. This sends little whales into a spin.

## Sink or Swim

The first thing a newborn whale must do is go to the surface for air, even though it is awkward and needs help swimming. Its mother, and sometimes another female whale, will help it to the surface. Within about a half hour, the baby will be able to swim without help.

## BABY BLUES

Whale babies grow quickly on their mothers' rich milk. Blue whale babies grow the fastest of all. At birth, they can be as long as 23 feet and weigh as much as 2 tons. They will drink from 50 to 130 gallons of milk a day and gain 7 pounds an hour. Usually, blue whales grow until they are about 30 years old, and they live to be 60 to 80 years old.

# Marine Iguanas

These reptiles, unique to the Galápagos Islands, are not the most attractive creatures. In fact, Charles Darwin described them as "most disgusting, clumsy lizards" and "hideous-looking"!

## Island Variety

Marine iguanas are generally dark gray or black, but the color varies depending on the island. They may have green, red, or gray patches. Española marine iguanas are the most colorful, with a combination of red, green, and black, earning them the nickname "Christmas iguanas."

## I'm Blushing

Male marine iguanas become more colorful during breeding season, with some turning almost completely red. During this time, the iguanas, like nearly all other reptiles, return to land.

## DID YOU KNOW?

Marine iguanas frequently sneeze to remove extra salt from their bodies. The spray of salt sometimes lands on their heads, leaving them with a white "wig."

## DEEP-SEA DIVER

The marine iguana of the Galápagos Islands is the only lizard truly at home in the sea. A vegetarian with little to choose from on the island, the iguana dives as deep as 30 feet to find seaweed and algae. While diving for food, the marine iguana can stop its heart completely for three minutes in order to save oxygen.

## Watery Living

While this iguana may not be skilled at walking on land, it is uniquely built for life in the water. A long, crocodile-like tail allows it to swim gracefully through the ocean, and a short snout and razor-sharp teeth are perfect for scraping algae off of rocks.

217

# Sounds of the Sea

Is that an orchestra under the sea? The musical monikers of common fish would suggest that the ocean serves as a concert hall, but unfortunately that is not the case. While some fish are named for the sounds they make, other fish are named for their resemblance to their namesake instruments.

## Nature's Vacuum

The trumpet fish often hides upright in the coral and swoops down from above to vacuum up its prey. Its ability to change color to match its surroundings catches prey off guard.

## Mooching Meals

Some trumpet fish search for prey by sneaking behind fish such as parrot fish or surgeonfish that are actively searching for and eating algae. The trumpet fish will then have an easy meal of small fish and invertebrates that are startled by the larger fish.

## STRING THEORY

Fiddler rays, sometimes called banjo rays or banjo sharks, are a genus of guitarfish. This species gets its name because its shape is similar to those string instruments—not from any musical talent!

## Drum Roll!

Underwater music gets its beat from the drumfish that vibrates its bladder to make the noise it's named for—a drumming sound—and it can be loud. A school of drums playing around a ship can keep a crew up all night!

## LONG NOSE

Flutemouth fish, or cornetfish, can grow up to 6.6 feet long. A large proportion of their bodies is taken up by their exceptionally long snouts. Like the trumpet fish, flutemouths use the suction in their snouts to vacuum unaware prey.

## Musical Sport

The red drum or redfish is one of the most popular recreational sport fish in coastal waters from Mexico to Massachusetts. It is one of the most widespread estuarine fish in Florida.

# So Many Sea Horses

## POT BELLY

The big-belly sea horse is one of the largest sea horse species and can grow to be about 14 inches long. This species has a big, round belly and is often called the potbellied sea horse because of it. Both males and females have this feature, but males are the only ones who will use it to carry offspring.

## Getting Warmer

Big-belly sea horses are very popular in Chinese medicine, the pet trade, and for use as decoration and jewelry. They are hard to keep alive in aquariums, however, because they require very specific temperatures to survive. They like water that is 70° to 80°F. Anything colder than that hurts their chances of survival.

## Eggstra Delivery

The spiny sea horse gets its name from the spines that run down its neck. Along with the distinctive spines, the spiny sea horse has a very long snout with white bars or dots running along it. The color of the spiny sea horse varies depending on its surroundings and can range from bright yellow to pale pink to green. While most sea horses lay around 200 babies, the spiny sea horse has been known to produce up to 581 offspring at once.

# CORAL CAMO

The pygmy sea horse is so good at camouflaging itself among the gorgonian coral where it lives that the species wasn't even discovered until the coral was being examined by scientists in a lab! Large, bulbous tubercles cover the sea horse's body, and they match the color and shape of the gorgonian coral exactly.

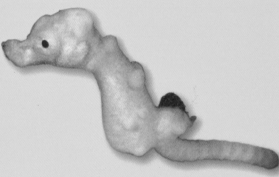

## Toy Horse

Pygmy sea horses only reach a length of 1 inch. Adults are usually found in pairs or clusters of pairs with up to 28 of these tiny sea horses recorded on a single coral. They only live in gorgonian coral in the tropical waters of the western Pacific Ocean, around Australia, Indonesia, Japan, New Caledonia, Papua New Guinea, and the Philippines.

## Zebra Snout

Barbour's sea horse, also known as the zebra snout sea horse, is the only sea horse species to be found exclusively in Southeast Asia in areas around Indonesia, Malaysia, and the Philippines. These sea horses are a shallow water species and can be found mainly in seagrass beds, mangrove swamps, estuaries, and muddy water less than 30 feet deep.

# Mudskippers

Mudskippers live along coasts, in estuaries and mangroves, and in swamps across Southeast Asia, Africa, and Australasia. These amphibious fish typically live near brackish water, a mix of freshwater and salt water.

## Fish Out of Water

The frog-faced mudskipper keeps its head above water. It seals water and air around its gills and returns to the water now and then to fill up. The mudskipper struts along with its pectoral fins and even leaps by pushing off the ground with its tail.

Mudskippers may spend up to **80%** of their time **on land.**

## Googly Goggles

Those googly eyes are protected by a layer of clear skin. A mudskipper will periodically roll its eyes back into their sockets to help keep them moist.

Gold-spotted mudskipper

# Pair Matching

## Poisonous Partners

There are 3 types of ocean residents below:
sea nettles, men o' war, and stingrays.
Draw a line to connect each of the 3 pairs
of identical twins.

  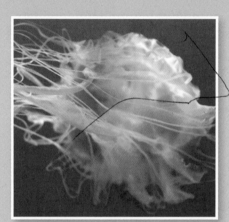

Answers on page 312

# Baby Boom

To reproduce, fish spawn—the female places her eggs in the water, the male releases sperm, and the eggs are fertilized. Most fish simply lay eggs and go on their way, but not all: Some build nests, dig pits, and find hiding places for their eggs. Eggs are good food for predators, but they are also the future for each fish species, so their survival is an important part of the fish story.

## Countless Cod

Fish that lay few eggs usually guard them, or none may survive. The cod can lay 4 million or more eggs a year, and the parents just let them float away without so much as a tail-wave goodbye. Only one baby in every million needs to live to continue the survival of this fish. If they all survived, the seas would be clogged with cod.

## SAFEKEEPING

An egg without any protection has a good chance of being eaten. Some sharks and skates lay their eggs in leathery cases. Each case is the home of just one egg, and the case has hooks that catch onto seaweed or anchor on the bottom of the ocean. There it sits for several months while the egg develops safely into a fish.

# Toadfish Treasure

Broken bottles, tin cans, boards, and plastic bottles—none of these belong on the ocean floor, but the toadfish is glad they are. This fish thinks litter is an ideal nesting site. The male toadfish guards the nest ferociously. His treasure is hidden in the trash.

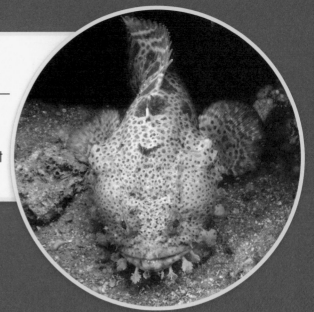

## Surf and Birth

The grunion rides the waves onto the beach. The female digs herself, tail first, into the soft, wet sand and lays her eggs. When she struggles free, the male fertilizes them. Then they both wiggle towards the sea and catch a wave into deeper water. Two weeks later a high tide washes the eggs out. Two or three minutes in the water and the baby grunions are hatched and swimming on their own.

## Egg-laying Champion

The ocean sunfish can measure 12 feet from top to bottom and weigh 3,000 pounds. It lays more eggs than any other fish—as many as 300 million eggs at a time.

# Sargasso Sea

The Sargasso Sea is a vast region of still, warm water in the North Atlantic Ocean. It is named for a genus of seaweed called sargassum that grows there..

## A Garden Grows

Sargassum seaweed gathers together and creates a free-floating garden that drifts along just below the surface. The seaweed reproduces vegetatively, meaning new seaweed is born from a single parent without any seeds or spores. Some types of sargassum have gas-filled bladders that act like buoys or floats.

## DID YOU KNOW?

The Sargasso Sea is the only sea in the world that is not surrounded by land! A system of ocean currents called a gyre acts as a boundary instead.

## Turtle Nursery

Sargassum serves as an important nursery for fledgling sea turtles such as loggerhead, green, and hawksbill turtles. It provides them with food and shelter.

# BIG BILLS

Billfish such as white marlins and blue marlins can be found in the Sargasso Sea. Billfish are some of the biggest and fastest predators in the sea.

**Dolphinfish, bluefin tuna, and humpback whales add to the diversity of species found in the Sargasso Sea.**

## PLANTING TRAPS

Sargassum fish have amazing camouflage. When they swim among the sargassum weed, they can make themselves look exactly like the plants. This trick helps them to catch unsuspecting prey.

# What's in a Name?

Fish have scientific names which place them in families so they can be studied in groups with similar characteristics. They also have common names. Here are some fish that have good reasons for their common names. They're funny, odd, peculiar, weird, and their names say it all.

**Trigger**

## Triggerfish

The triggerfish has a fin-shaped trigger, and it actually works. The trigger is created by locking the spines of its dorsal fin. When a triggerfish is frightened, it dives into coral and uses its spine to anchor itself where enemies can't reach it. To be safe, this fish has to be quick on the trigger.

## FLATHEAD

The hammerhead shark has a head like a flattened bar—hammer's head—with an eye and a nostril on each end. Other fish must wonder where the hammerhead is looking.

## Filefish

Some fish are named for their shape, but the filefish is named for its skin. The skin of this fish is so hard and rough, it has been used as sandpaper—an unusual fish!

# NEEDLEFISH

Needlefish are silvery, skinny, and about 6 feet long. Slicing through the surface of the water, they look like floating needles. The needlefish uses its sharp teeth to snatch small fish and juggle them into a head-first position in its mouth. Then—slurp!—it swallows them whole.

# Cowfish

The smallest creature to be called a cow has got to be the cowfish. Only 1 foot long, this fish got its name from the two cowlike horns that stick out of its head.

# Mackerel Sharks

The order Lamniformes is a group of sharks called mackerels. Mackerel sharks tend to look like what we think of as the "typical" shark, menacing and vicious, like the great white shark. However, this order also includes more docile, or gentle, species like the sand tiger shark, as well as filter feeders like the megamouth shark.

## SCARY SELLS

Sand tiger sharks, also known as graynurse sharks and sand tigers, were first known as sand sharks, due to their tendency to live on the ocean floor near the shore. The word "tiger" may have been added because of their big appetites, but it's also rumored that aquariums decided to change the name to make them sound more ferocious! Despite jagged teeth and a scary appearance, sand tiger sharks aren't very aggressive to people. These sharks tend to leave people alone unless people bother them first.

## Big Babies

A female sand tiger shark carries eggs that hatch inside her body. The first embryo, or fertilized egg, to hatch will begin eating its underdeveloped brothers and sisters. When two dominating baby sand sharks remain, they move on to eat their mother's unfertilized eggs. That's how they grow—and grow. By the time they are born, the babies are almost half the size of their mother!

# SWORD SWALLOWER

The mako is powerful and thought to be dangerous. It is the fastest shark of all, clocked at 43 miles per hour. It is known to leap out of water—sometimes into boats! The mako seems to have very little fear: A large, 730-pound mako was once caught with a 120-pound swordfish in its stomach—sword and all!

## Mighty Mellow

The appropriately named megamouth shark is very rare and has been sighted fewer than 20 times since its discovery in 1976. Its large body and small, soft fins make it a poor swimmer, and it is not as menacing as it sounds. The megamouth stays in the depths of the ocean during the day and migrates towards the surface to feed on plankton. It has about 50 rows of teeth but only uses the first three to filter its food.

Sand tiger sharks are the only known sharks to pop up to the surface, but they don't do this to breathe like marine mammals would. Instead, they gulp in air into their stomachs to help them float motionless in the water as they look for prey.

# Blue Button and Moon Jellyfish

## Colony Life

The blue button jellyfish isn't a true jellyfish! It consists of a hydroid colony of polyps surrounding a float. The float is golden or brown, round, flat, and about 1 inch wide. The colony of polyps can range in color from turquoise to yellow. It consists of tentacles with numerous branchlets containing stinging cells at their ends. The sting of the blue button jellyfish is not very powerful, but it can cause some minor irritation on human skin.

## Beach Float

Blue button jellyfish normally float through the ocean using ocean currents and wind. They travel in large groups and can sometimes be found beached on the shore.

## Bottoms Up

Blue button jellyfish feed on both living and dead organisms. They mainly eat fish eggs, small fish, larvae, and zooplankton. Each jellyfish has a single mouth located on the bottom of the float. It uses it for both taking in nutrients and getting rid of waste.

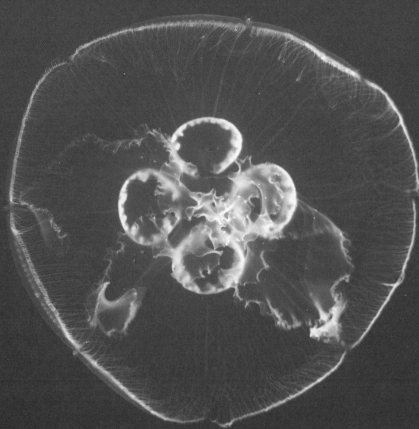

## Clear as a Bell

Moon jellyfish are named for their translucent, circular bells that resemble the moon. Unlike many species of jellyfish, moon jellyfish have a short, fine fringe that sweeps food towards a layer of mucus on the edge of the bell. Prey is stored in pouches until the jellyfish's oral arms pick it up and digest it.

## QUIET LIVES

Moon jellies are found throughout the world in both temperate and tropical waters. They feed in quiet bays and harbors and pose very little threat to humans, even though they do have the ability to sting.

## Colorful Diet

The moon jellyfish changes colors based on what it has been eating. If it is pink or lavender, it means it has been eating crustaceans. An orange tint signals a diet of brine shrimp.

# That Stings!

## Spine Story

A stingray, like most rays and skates, lies in shallow water covered with sand and minds its own business—unless someone steps on it. Then—whap!—it swings its long tail and strikes with its spine. The single spine on the tail of a stingray is poisonous and dangerous. Depending on the size of the ray, the wound it causes can be merely painful or totally paralyzing. Some rays even have spines that are replaced if they are lost.

Stingrays eat clams, oysters, shrimp, crabs, and mussels. They crush their prey using their **strong jaws.**

## Rays Around the World

Lurking in coastal waters around the world are more than 100 kinds of stingrays. Some grow very large, weighing well over 600 pounds, sometimes with a fin span of more than 10 feet.

# Maze

## Rockin' Rays

These 2 rays are hunting for a meal.
Help the manta ray get to the
plankton and the stingray find
a fish in the sand.

# Tube Blennies

Blenny is the common name for the hundreds of species belonging to two suborders: Blennioidei, or blennies, and Notothenioidei, known as Antarctic blennies.

## Mood Swings

**Blennies have different temperaments depending on the species. They can range from calm to aggressive. It doesn't matter what size they are, either. Some very small blennies are the most aggressive!**

## All by Myself

Blennies are typically very reclusive. They hide on the ocean floor, in reefs, rocks, or kelp, in burrows or discarded shells and bottles, and in eelgrass or algae.

# Meal Mystery

Scientists don't know much about the feeding habits of the sarcastic fringehead, but they think that the fish's large mouth makes it hard for them to feed properly. Most blennies will feed on plankton, but the sarcastic fringehead is unable to suction feed.

# In the Tubes

The sarcastic fringehead lives off the coast of California in the northeast Pacific Ocean. Sarcastic fringeheads are considered tube blennies because they live in burrows or tube structures.

# Competitive Streak

Female sarcastic fringeheads look for male partners that will be good protectors, since males must guard the female's eggs until they hatch. This means males are extremely aggressive when competing for mates. A male sarcastic fringehead opens his mouth wide in his rivals' direction, which lets the larger male establish dominance over smaller fish.

# Blue and Fin Whales

## BIG HEART

The blue whale is the largest animal to ever have lived. It reaches an average length of 79 to 88½ feet and a weight of 110 to 132 tons. The largest blue whale ever recorded was 110 feet long! The heart of a blue whale is about the size of a Volkswagen Beetle!

## Can You Hear Me?

Blue whales have the loudest calls of any animal on Earth. They produce a variety of low frequency sounds and clicks. The male blue whale makes an especially long call, which scientists think functions as a way to sense the environment, detect prey, communicate, and as a male display.

## Natural Filter

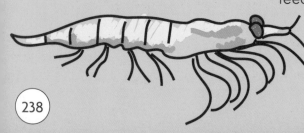

The blue whale is a baleen whale, which means that it filter feeds. Each whale has 300 to 400 black baleen plates on each side of its mouth and about 90 throat grooves that allow the throat of the whale to enormously expand during feeding. The blue whale can consume up to 40 million krill per day during the summer feeding season!

## SECOND PLACE

Fin whales are the second largest whale and are known as the greyhounds of the sea. They can reach speeds of about 22 miles per hour. These whales can reach a length of nearly 79 feet and weigh between 50 to 70 tons!

## Only Child

A female fin whale gestates, or is pregnant, for 11 months and will produce a single calf. This calf is nursed for six to eight months. When the calf is weaned, it will be between 33 to 40 feet long.

## Ships in the Night

Fin whales are split into two subspecies, one in the Northern Hemisphere and the other in the Southern Hemisphere. These two species never seem to come into contact with each other because the seasonal patterns in each hemisphere are opposites, meaning northern and southern whales migrate to the equator at different times of the year. Fin whales spend spring and early summer in cold feeding groups at high latitudes and migrate to warmer southern waters for the winter and the breeding season.

# Beautiful Butterflies

Butterfly fish come in a wide range of colors and patterns and are one of the most common sights on coral reefs around the world. Some species have dull coloring, but most species are brightly colored with interesting patterns. At night, when the butterfly fish settles into the dark crevices where it hides, its brilliant colors and markings fade to blend in with the background.

## CLOSE COUSINS

There are over 100 species of butterfly fish. They all have thin, disc-shaped bodies and closely resemble their cousins the angelfish. Some species are solitary, while others travel in small schools. When the butterfly fish finds a partner, the pair tends to mate for life.

Don't confuse me! I'm an angelfish!

## Pair Up

Raccoon butterfly fish are nocturnal. They can be found in pairs or small groups in shallow reef flats and ocean reefs. Raccoon butterfly fish eat mainly nudibranchs, tube worm tentacles, and other invertebrates, including algae and coral polyps.

# Eye Spy

The foureye butterfly fish gets its name from the eyespots on its tail that it uses to confuse predators. If the fish cannot escape using trickery, it will face its foe, extend its dorsal spines, and attempt to intimidate the other animal. At the very least, it will remind the other animal that the butterfly fish is too spiny for predators to comfortably eat.

# Coral Crush

The spot-tail butterfly fish lives in coral-rich areas of reef flats, lagoons, and seaward reefs. Juvenile fish stay closer to the shore, but adults can be found at depths of 150 feet. They depend on coral reefs for food, so scientists are concerned about how declining coral reefs will affect them.

# Pest Control

Copperband butterfly fish are desirable not only for their lovely appearance, but for a particular habit: This fish is known to consume aiptasia, anemones considered pests in tanks.

# Ocean Fruits

## BERRY RED

Because of its popularity, the brilliant-red strawberry hermit crab is endangered in Australia and has been protected by law from harvesting for the pet trade. Currently, most of the strawberry hermit crabs sold as pets in the United States come from Malaysia and Indonesia, where they aren't currently endangered.

## Roughed Up

The berry sponge, also known as the golf ball sponge, is found in reefs off the coast of New Zealand in shaded areas on rock walls or under seaweed. This coin-sized sponge is scaly and has a rough texture.

## Trash Collectors

**Strawberry hermit crabs are known as the garbage collectors of the seashore, because they will eat various dead and rotting materials along the shore.**

## Opportunity Knocks

Citron coral gobies are planktivores, animals that feed on plankton. These fish are considered opportunistic feeders, not hunters. Instead of actively searching for food, the gobies wait for food to come into range, dart out to grab it, and quickly return to their roosts.

## NUT JOB

Coconut octopuses are veined octopuses that use coconut shells as tools to protect themselves from predators. Scientists first observed this practice in Indonesia. Octopuses dug up two halves of a coconut and carried them around to use as defense from predators when they were resting in sediment or stopping in an exposed area. Carrying the shell halves is awkward for the octopus and slows the animal down, but the protection that comes from hiding inside the shell makes it all worthwhile.

## Organ Defense

The pineapple sea cucumber uses the knobby bumps on its body for protection. Like many sea cucumbers, it can expel its internal organs when threatened. The organs will entangle or distract the predator so that the cucumber can escape.

## Get Red-dy

The cherry barb is a deep red color that intensifies during mating season in males. Wild-caught cherry barbs have a brighter color than those bred in captivity.

243

# Giants

## What a Hog

The giant hogfish gets its name from its long, piglike snout and its jaw that extends to root around the bottom of the sea floor. Giant hogfish can grow up to about 40 inches long and weigh 20 pounds. The hogfish is a popular fish to catch due to its unique taste, but this has led to overfishing and made the hogfish a vulnerable species.

## HAWK HUNGER

The distinct markings on the giant hawkfish make it easy to identify. It likes to hide in coral and rocky reefs close to shore while waiting to capture a delicious meal of small fish and crustaceans wandering near its lair.

## FROG MOUTH

Giant frogfish are sneaky feeders. They can change color to blend in with their surroundings and catch their prey by surprise. A frogfish mostly eats small fish, but its mouth can expand up to 12 times its normal size, which allows it to catch fish much larger than itself. If waiting for prey to swim by isn't working, the giant frogfish uses its fleshy "lure" to draw them in.

# SLAM DUNK

The giant basket star is a nocturnal species. When the basket star goes to feed at night, it faces into the current and opens its numerous arms to form a net to catch plankton. When an arm catches food, it curls towards the basket star's mouth so the star can take a bite. During the day, the basket star curls into a ball under coral to avoid detection.

# BAD RAP

**Giant moray eels have a bad reputation that is largely unearned. They are thought of as vicious or bad-tempered, but, in reality, they would rather hide from humans and flee instead of fight. The eels only attack humans in self-defense or when they mistake human for food.**

# JAWS

The giant moray eel is the largest of the eel species and can reach a length of 9.8 feet and a weight of 66 pounds. This eel has a feature that makes it unique among all other animals: It has a second set of jaws at the back of its throat. This set of jaws works to hold caught prey and pull it into the eel's digestive tract.

# The Professionals

These sea creatures all have professional titles.

## Exterior Decorator

Decorator crabs won't help you pick out a new couch, but they do have amazing camouflage skills! They pick out seaweed, anemones, sponges, and bryozoans, a type of invertebrates, from their habitat and attach them to their shells using hooked setae, which resembles velcro bristles. Like most crabs, decorators shed their shells as they grow.

### DID YOU KNOW?

Decorator crabs will take decorations from their old shells and reattach them to the new shells they've grown.

## Make Yourself at Home

Decorator crabs don't always get to choose the decorations on their backs. Once a crab has grown large enough to protect itself, it doesn't pick out plants and animals for its shell. However, plants and animals will often settle on the shell without help, take hold, and grow on their own.

# FORWARD MARCH

Soldier crabs are unique in their ability to move forwards, instead of sideways like every other crab species. When they march along the beach, they sift through the sand for dead bits of plants and animals to eat. They discard the sand in little balls, leaving paths behind them.

## SCHOOL DROP-OFF

The schoolmaster snapper gets its name from its habit of gathering in dense schools of fish. As juveniles, schoolmaster snappers tend to stay close to land in shallow coastal waters. As they age, the fish migrate a little deeper to gather around coral or shallow wrecks. The biggest schoolmasters stay near the drop-offs of coral reefs.

# NICE NURSE

The nurse shark isn't your usual fearsome shark. It feeds on bottom invertebrates like spiny lobsters, shrimp, crabs, sea urchins, squids, and octopuses, as well as fish. The nurse shark also has the ability to create a vacuum with its mouth to suck prey out of hiding and even snails from their shells!

# Recycling

Sometimes scientists reuse animal names
to create new ones for other species.

## Spiny Waspfish

The uncommon spiny waspfish can be easily overlooked on the sandy bottoms of the coastal slope where it lives. It mimics the sway of floating leaves or rubble in the water to avoid detection. The waspfish's coloring helps it remain well-hidden, too. These fish are different shades of brown flecked with white, so it blends with the bottom where it dwells.

## Tiger Shark

Tiger sharks get their name from the dark stripes on their sides, which are most distinct on juvenile sharks and fade with age. These creatures have a reputation as ferocious man-eaters, but they have a less fearsome nickname—"wastebasket of the sea." This name comes from their habit of swallowing anything they come across—even garbage.

## Lizard Fish

There are about 50 species of lizard fish that can be found mainly in tropical areas. One species found in Hawaii has a strange mouth—even its tongue is lined with teeth! Once it bites its prey, it isn't letting go!

## Sea Raven

Sea ravens are sometimes considered the balloons of the ocean because of their habit of sucking in huge amounts of water without the ability to quickly expel it. The water-filled fish will float around, using their tails to steer until the water can be naturally released. Scientists aren't yet sure why these animals can't deflate themselves.

# Word Scramble

## Watery Words

Unscramble the letters to find the names of some interesting sea animals.

LOCICA   BACR

— — — — — —   — — — —

INF   HAELW

— — —   — — — — —

AZDLRI   IFHS

— — — — — —   — — — —

TANIG   FIHORFGS

— — — — —   — — — — — — — —

TEMHMOGUA   KHASR

— — — — — — — — —   — — — — —

KASHIBLWL   RUTTEL

— — — — — — — — —   — — — — — —

ONOCTUC   TOPOCSU

— — — — — — —   — — — — — — —

GYPYM   ESA   SHEOR

— — — — —   — — —   — — — — —

DOSIREL   BACR

— — — — — — —   — — — —

# Whale Social Life

## Home, Home on the Sea

Whales and dolphins live in all the world's oceans, and some of its rivers as well. Some live far out to sea while others hug the shore.

Orcas close to shore

## Invisible Maps

Whales and dolphins navigate by following the hills and valleys on the ocean floor, by racking the sun, by sensing ocean currents, and by tasting the water from rivers and bays along their journey. They also detect changes in Earth's magnetic field, a sense that acts like an internal compass. This "compass" helps them through even dark, murky water.

# BUDDY BAILOUT

Dolphins swim in large herds that sometimes number over 1,000 individuals. They also associate with whales, such as the right, humpback, and gray whales. Within these groups, dolphins look out for one another. When danger approaches, they send signals. If one member is injured or in distress, they push it to the surface so it can breathe.

# Round-trip Travelers

Many whales migrate constantly, traveling from one region to another to find food, breed, and have their young. Each spring, gray whales leave their winter breeding grounds off the coast of Baja California. They head to the Arctic Ocean, where they feed on krill. In September, they start south again, swimming 24 hours a day to reach their favorite lagoons in time to have their young. The round-trip journey is over 12,000 miles.

# Ocean Royalty

## Kingdom of Angels

Emperor angelfish have kingdoms to match their titles: An angelfish territory can be over 10,000 square feet! Male emperor angelfish are very protective of their habitats and will defend their living space and the females living with them.

Adult emperor angelfish

Juvenile emperor angelfish

## Queen's Quarters

When it's time to sleep, queen parrot fish and other parrot fish species get cozy in cocoon-like structures made of their own mucus. Scientists believe this helps to mask their scent, providing some protection against predators and parasites.

Queen parrot fish are an important species in their environment. When they eat certain species of algae, they only digest the soft parts. The hard parts they pass create much of the sand around a reef. Eating algae also leaves more open surfaces for coral to attach to and grow.

*Pseudanthias pascalus* male

*Pseudanthias tuka* male

# Who's the QUEEN?

Two very similar species of fish in the same genus, *Pseudanthias*, have caused scientists quite a bit of confusion in the game of who's who. *Pseudanthias pascalus* is sometimes called the amethyst anthias or sailfin basslet, and *Pseudanthius tuka* goes by yellowstriped fairy basslet or purple anthias, but both species claim the title of purple queen. The females are easier to tell apart, because *P. tuka* has a yellow stripe along her back while *P. pascalus* is all purple. Because color varies so much in males depending on the region, it is difficult to distinguish the species.

# ROYAL ROLL CALL

The queen coris drastically changes in appearance throughout its life. When young, the fish is orange with white stripes along its body. As it ages, it transforms into a whole new fish! Females become dark blue-green with black spots and red on their fins, and the males have blue stripes on light blue bodies and green stripes on their faces.

# Regal Appetite

**The talang queenfish of the Indian and west Pacific Oceans is a predator with a large appetite. Its mouth is full of sharp teeth that help it devour its meals of crabs, squids, and small fish.**

# Penguins on the Map

## Pint-sized Penguin

The shy little penguin can be found on the coasts of New Zealand, Australia, and some surrounding islands. Also known as the fairy penguin, this bird is the smallest of all penguins at around 1 foot tall and less than 3 pounds. Little penguins don't migrate like some other penguins, instead traveling only about 1/3 mile between their nests and the sea. It's a short but risky trip, threatened by the likes of cats, dogs, weasels, and even cars.

## Hot and Cold

Galápagos penguins make their nests on the Galápagos Islands, off the coast of South America. That's nearly on the equator—a very hot spot! The ocean there is cold, however, fed by a current flowing from the icy Antarctic—and filled with the foods that penguins like to eat.

## Cool Off

In warm places, such as the Galápagos Islands, penguins need to cool off. Feather fluffing is the answer. Penguins can lift their feathers and keep them up, so air can cool their skin. They also stick out their winglike flippers to help heat escape.

## Bouncing Birds

Rockhoppers build nests on steep, rocky areas that they reach by jumping. With both feet held together, they bounce 4 to 5 feet from one ledge to another. Rockhopper penguins live along shorelines of the islands north of Antarctica. Macaroni penguins build their nests on steep, rough ground, too. Sometimes they build on lava flows, rock slopes, and in caves.

Rockhopper penguin

I'm still ALIVE!

## BIRD WATCHING

The first time Europeans set eyes on a penguin was when explorer Vasco da Gama sailed down the coast of Africa in 1497. One surprised sailor reported that he saw birds that made a sound like a mule and couldn't fly. Over 500 years later, the black-footed penguin is still living on the coasts and small islands around the southern tip of Africa.

## Rain Forest Express

The Fiordland penguin, also known as the tawaki, is a crested penguin at home on South Island in New Zealand. Tawakis raise their young in the rain forest, safe from any natural ground predators. Every day, the adults travel back and forth to the sea to feed, using streams as convenient expressways.

## Yellow-eyed

The yellow-eyed is one of the tallest penguins. A bit different from the black-and-white variety of penguins, the yellow-eyed has a slate-blue back, white undersides, and striking yellow eyes. This penguin can be found in New Zealand and on nearby islands.

# Tricky Fish

Tricky fish! They walk. They talk. They breathe and fly. They even hibernate. Who are they and how did they get this way? Slowly. The oldest fish fossil found so far is over 500 million years old. Over the centuries, as fish changed and adapted to their surroundings, some of them developed bizarre, fantastic behaviors.

## WALKING UNDERWATER

Watch a sea robin move along the ocean floor, and it seems to be walking. Six rays, three from each pectoral fin, stick out and poke around in the sand.

## Take Cover

Here comes the archerfish squirting bullets. Insects are its prey, and water is its weapon. Spotting a bug on a leaf, the archerfish gets in position, takes aim, and shoots drops of water at its victim. A sure shot at 4 feet, larger archerfish can propel water up to 12 feet.

# Flying Hatchet

Meet the only true flyer among fish, the tiny, 3-inch hatchet fish, shaped like a food chopper. Whizzing along for about 6 feet, flapping its pectoral fins like mad, this fish actually flies! Huge chest muscles, a quarter of its weight, give the hatchet the power to take off.

Remora

# Free Ride

A remora doesn't look too strange until you notice the powerful suction disc on top of its head. The disc lets the remora stick to animals like sharks or turtles. The fish gets a free ride, plus any food that the larger animal drops. Now that's using its head!

# Shark Dining

## Feeding Frenzy

Sharks normally dine alone, but sometimes they have a vicious party—a feeding frenzy. One feeding shark may attract others. Racing to the scene, they slash at the prey and bite wildly at anything that gets in their way—even each other. Then, it's over as quickly as it began.

## ∽ On the Menu ∽

Eating to survive is the name of the game in the ocean, and sharks are the champs.

Some sharks eat:
PLANKTON, MOLLUSKS and CRUSTACEANS (like snails and shrimp)
at the bottom of the ocean.

Then there are those that eat larger prey, such as:
SEALS, TURTLES, SEAGULLS, AND DOLPHINS.

Great white shark

# Messy Eater

Sharks bite, but they do not chew. They swallow things whole or in big pieces. Some use their teeth like a fork and knife—they have pointed teeth in the lower jaw to puncture prey, and serrated teeth in the top to saw away at meat.

## SHARK EAT SHARK

Sharks don't just eat other sea creatures. They also eat each other. Once, a tiger shark was caught with a bull shark in its stomach. In the bull shark's belly, scientists found a blacktip shark. And the blacktip's stomach revealed a dogfish shark!

**Think of sharks, and you picture sharp, pointed teeth. Study sharks, and you'll find that there are many different kinds of teeth. Shark teeth are so unique that scientists can identify sharks by them—or by the bite they leave behind.**

# Dental Plan

Sharks have a lifetime supply of teeth, with rows and rows set in soft tissue. An adult probably goes through seven to 12 sets in one year. Each time a tooth is lost by biting or through aging, a new tooth moves forward and takes its place.

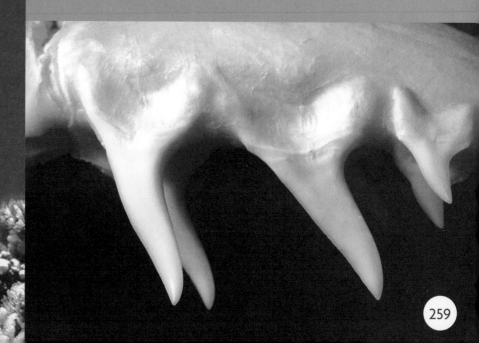

# Puffed Up

Who is that spiky ball swimming in the ocean? It's a puffer fish! Puffer fish are not always round—they can look like ordinary fish until they are in danger. Then they are able to inflate their bodies with water, turning them into round, spiky balls that are nearly impossible for predators to swallow.

Puffer fish have four teeth that are fused to form a beak. This beak is very strong. Puffer fish use it to crack open clams and mussels.

Not all puffer fish have spikes, but all puffer fish do **INFLATE** their bodies to several times their normal size.

## DID YOU KNOW?

Swallowing a puffer fish before it inflates is a bad idea: The puffer not only tastes terrible but is also poisonous and will most likely kill the fish that tries to eat it!

Some sharks are **immune** to a puffer fish's poison—that means they can **eat** a puffer fish and be fine.

# The Tale of Tails

Whales and dolphins propel themselves through the water with their tails, which have two strong wings, or flukes. Instead of wagging their flukes from side to side like fish, they move them up and down in powerful strokes.

The blue whale's 16-foot flukes are relatively small for such an enormous animal.

A sperm whale's huge, triangular flukes are 13 feet across.

Sometimes a humpback whale uses its powerful flukes to catapult right out of the water!

Humpback whale

## Fabulous Flippers

A whale has a flipper on each side at the front of its body. Before whales moved into the water, these flippers were actually legs that were used for walking on land. Whale flippers are now used for steering, braking, and sometimes to knock away attackers—but not for swimming.

# FINTASTIC

A stiff fin on the back of most whales helps the mammal stay on course while swimming. Depending on the whale, this dorsal fin can be small or large.

A killer whale's dorsal fin can grow up to 6 feet.

The beluga is one of the few whales without a dorsal fin.

The huge fin whale has a tiny dorsal fin.

# Sea Pens

A sea pen is a colony of polyps working together to survive. The original polyp loses its tentacles and becomes the stalk of the pen, attaching its bulb to the ocean floor. Secondary polyps act as branches of the pen, and each one has a certain job: Some catch plankton to feed the pen; some reproduce; and some move the water that ventilates the colony.

When the sea pen is disturbed, it will force water out of the colony. This makes it possible for it to retract into the bulbous foot of the pen. When sea pens are stimulated, they glow with a bright greenish light.

The sea pen got its name from its resemblance to an old-fashioned quill pen. These creatures can be a variety of colors, ranging from dark orange to blue to white.

# Spot the Difference
## Sea Pen Pandemonium

Find and circle 5 differences between these two pictures of sea pens.

Answers on page 315

# Jewels

The emerald crab lives in coral and under rocks in shallow water of 8 to 10 feet. The texture of the crab mimics the rough surroundings and helps the crab defend itself.

I'm fine!

## Clingy

The tiny emerald crab only grows to be about 1½ inches, but its small size doesn't prevent it from being a tough crab. In the wild, it has been shown to live in ocean conditions that are too harsh or variable for other animals. These crabs tolerate extreme temperatures on both ends of the thermometer and can live in areas of heavy surges due to their ability to cling onto things.

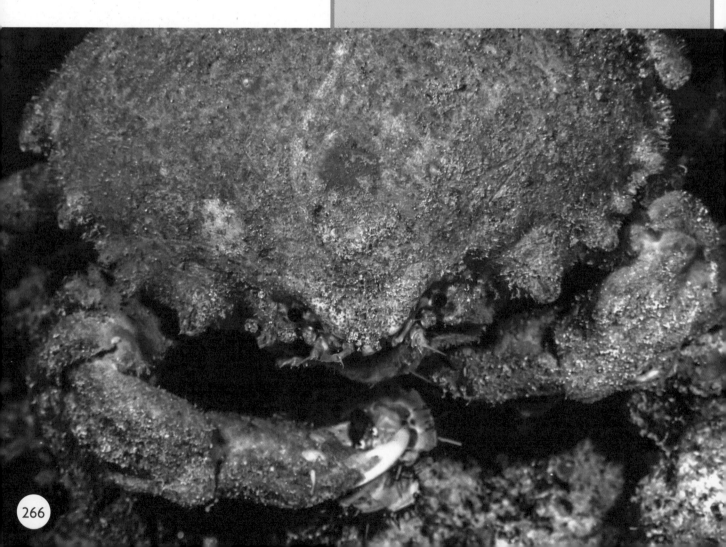

## Rainbow Scales

The scales of the pearlscale butterfly fish create a rainbow effect, and the black edges create a cross-hatched pattern—adding up to one lovely fish! The fish's eye is camouflaged by a black stripe, and a vertical orange stripe runs down the tail.

## Slime Time

Jewel puffer fish are a very slimy species. They secrete mucus from their skin to protect against parasites and infections, as well as to help them move through the water faster.

The jewel puffer fish is also known as the false eye toby, because, as the name suggests, it has a false eye on its rear dorsal fin to confuse predators.

## Key Species

Atlantic silversides are important in the food chain and to scientists. In the wild, they are prey to many predatory fish, such as mackerel, bass, and bluefish, as well as many birds like terns and cormorants. Scientists use them for research purposes because they are sensitive to environmental conditions like low oxygen levels, temperature changes, and water contamination.

# Looks Like Christmas

Christmas tree worms live on tropical coral reefs around the world at depths of less than 100 feet. These worms seem to prefer certain coral species more than others, and scientists still aren't sure why this is. Some scientists think specific types of coral help with reproduction, while others think the preference of these corals has to do with avoiding predators that also inhabit coral, like parrot fish.

## Bunker Down

The Christmas tree worm has a pair of crowns that resemble Christmas trees! The crowns provide oxygen and filter out tiny plants and animals to eat, but they're only a small part of the worm—two-thirds of the worm's body hides inside a calcium carbonate tube to protect it from danger. Some species make homes within the living tissue of coral, forcing the polyps to build around them. These "bunkers" can reach 10 inches in length.

**Christmas tree worms have long lives. Although the average lifespan is 10 to 20 years, the worms can live up to 30 years once they choose a home.**

## Speed Breeding

Unlike many other invertebrates, there are both male and female Christmas tree worms. When Christmas tree worms reproduce, they shoot their genetic material into the surrounding water, hoping that it meets a match nearby. Once fertilization happens, larvae develop in only 24 hours.

## Testing the Waters

When these tiny creatures are startled, they retract into their bunkers and wait for the danger to pass. Christmas tree worms are easily startled—they retract at the lightest touch or a passing shadow. Typically, they will very slowly reemerge a minute later, testing the water before fully extending their plumes once more.

# We Are Family

Orca pods are very much like close families. An orca spends its whole life in the same group and continues to stay attached to its mother. Each pod may also have its own specific way of living, choosing to eat certain things and communicating in ways slightly different from other pods.

Found in all the world's oceans, from the tropics to the Arctic, orcas usually live in pods numbering three to 20, but sometimes they travel in larger herds that number 100.

# TEACHABLE

Orcas are very intelligent and can be trained for performances at marine parks. There is a lot of controversy about these shows and whether or not orcas should be in captivity.

# Orca Antics

Like dolphins, orcas love to play. Although they can weigh as much as 18,000 pounds and grow to 32 feet, they are very athletic. Orcas can swim 30 miles per hour and can leap and turn quickly. These talents are what make them so dangerous. They fear nothing and can chase down almost any sea creature.

## False Alarm

The false killer whale shares many characteristics with the orca, including appearance. However, it's a very large dolphin and is not remotely related to the killer whale. The false killer is the third largest dolphin in existence, averaging a length of 15 to 17 feet. Females are 1 to 3 feet shorter and weigh about 2,400 to 2,600 pounds.

Male

Female

# Fin Towers

How can you tell male and female orcas apart? Females—and young orcas—have smaller, curved dorsal fins that resemble those of dolphins, while male fins are much taller.

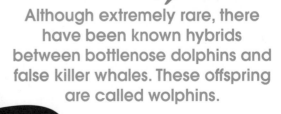

Although extremely rare, there have been known hybrids between bottlenose dolphins and false killer whales. These offspring are called wolphins.

# Ghost Pipefish and Cardinal Fish

## Strong Pipes

The ghost pipefish's head makes up 44% of its total body length. This species got its name from its long, tubelike snout that sucks up prey from the sea floor as it floats along vertically in an upside down position.

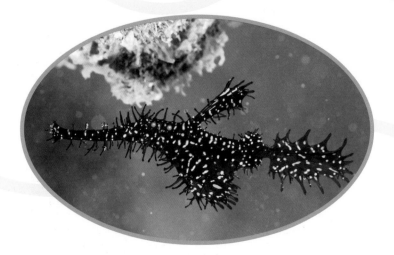

## Tiny Tots

Ghost pipefish are monogamous, which means they only have one mate at a time. Unlike true pipefish and sea horses, the female rather than the male incubates the eggs—up to 350 eggs at one time. These eggs develop while attached to specialized skin cells on the pipefish. When they hatch, the larvae are only 3 millimeters long.

## Seeing Ghosts

The ghost pipefish often lets itself be carried by the current and mimics a piece of dead seaweed in order to avoid detection. The pipefish is an ambush predator that floats along until it finds a meal of invertebrates.

## BLACK AND WHITE

The Banggai cardinal fish is a beautifully patterned fish. It has a shiny, silvery body with three black bars running vertically down its head and sides. Between those stripes are white dots uniquely patterned on each fish.

## Take Care

Female banggai cardinal fish choose their male partners for mating. Each pair moves to its own territory where the female lays eggs, and the male swallows and incubates the eggs in a special pouch in his mouth. The eggs remain in the pouch for several days after hatching, until they are 5 to 6 millimeters long. The male tends to the eggs while they are in his mouth and does not eat. After the male releases his offspring, he does not interact with them.

# Power Tools

## Sawtooth

The sawshark has teeth on the outside of its mouth. It has a long, flat, bladelike snout with teeth on either side, like a saw. Unborn sawsharks have soft teeth that are folded back until birth, when contact with salt water hardens them. This protects the mother carrying the baby shark inside her body.

## Hammered In

Having eyes and nostrils sometimes a yard apart, a hammerhead shark is able to sample a wide range of water at one time, sniffing out food as it swings its head from left to right. And, as if one weird head were not enough, there are many types of hammerheads.

## Razor Sharp

The pearly razorfish is not as dangerous as its name implies. Widespread throughout the Mediterranean Sea and parts of the Atlantic Ocean, these fish will dive headfirst into the sand when frightened.

## STRAIGHT-EDGED

Razor clams come by their name honestly: Their long, narrow shape resembles an old-fashioned, straight-edged razor! The shape makes the clams very sharp and allows them to burrow vertically in the sand. To swim, a razor clam uses a springlike motion, extending its foot, folding it back in, and straightening it once more to propel itself forward.

# Underwater Maze

## Cats of the Sea

Help the leopard shark get back to the seafloor. Make sure to avoid the tiger shark, which might just make the leopard shark its dinner!

Answers on page 316

# Feeling Crabby

The giant spider crab, also called the Japanese spider crab, is the world's largest known arthropod and is thought to be able to live up to 100 years.

## What makes this crab so enormous?

Its body stops growing once it reaches about 15 inches, but the legs keep growing and can measure 12 feet from claw to claw! This monstrous-looking crab can weigh up to 44 pounds.

## SETTLE DOWN

When giant spider crabs are in their larval stage, they are small, round, transparent, and legless. They float on the ocean surface and drift like plankton. When the crabs mature, they live at depths of 500 to 1,000 feet or more. They like to settle down near vents and holes on the ocean floor.

# Rock Bottom

The box crab has evolved to become a master of disguise, since it's a popular meal for octopuses and other bottom-dwelling creatures. The crab buries itself in the mud, pulling its legs under its body and folding its claws in front, giving it a box shape. When it lies still, it is nearly impossible to distinguish from the ocean bottom.

# Can Opener

The box crab's claws are specifically adapted to eating snails. The right claw has a hook and knobs that work like a can opener to remove the snail shell, and the left claw has a pointed pincer to grab the snail's body.

# Roommates

The anemone hermit crab lives in the Indo-Pacific region on coral reefs and in intertidal zones, and it has a symbiotic relationship with anemones. The hermit crab allows anemones to live on its shell, giving the anemones a better habitat, defense against predators, and food from the crab's messy meals. In return, the anemone helps to defend the crab against predators like octopuses.

# Natural Oddities

## Getting Attached

The lumpfish, also known as the lumpsucker, belongs to the family Cyclopteridae, which gets its name from the Greek words *kyklos*, meaning "round," and *pteron*, which means "fin." Instead of scales, these fish have three rows of large, bony protrusions, called tubercles. Lumpfish's pelvic fins act like suction discs, which allow the fish to attach themselves to rocks and other objects.

## Beard Burn

Bearded fireworms are flattened, segmented worms with groups of hollow, venom-filled bristles along each side. They are typically about 3 to 4 inches long, but can be as long as 14 inches. The bristles of the bearded fireworm penetrate the flesh of prey and break off inside, causing a burning, irritated area, and earning this species the name "fireworm."

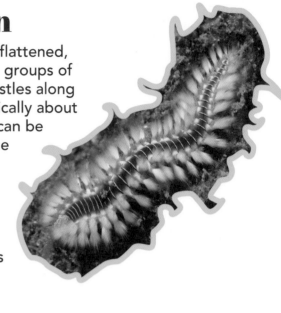

# Soapy Suds

There are about 24 species of soapfish, but the greater soapfish is the best-known of them all. It is found in the Atlantic Ocean and ranges from the southern United States to northern South America and West Africa. The soapfish gets its name from its ability to produce a toxic mucus that forms a slimy, sudsy froth in the water when the fish is agitated. This mucus is used to deter predators.

## All-day Buffet

The shorthorn sculpin is a very lazy fish. It often lies motionless on the bottom of the ocean, and, even though it loves to eat, rarely moves even several feet to catch bait dangling above it. Unlike other fish, it will not voluntarily come to the surface of the water.

Shorthorn sculpin eat a lot of food. They mainly eat crustaceans, like crabs, but will also dine on shrimp, sea urchins, worms, the fry of other fish, and sometimes even shellfish. They scavenge for food as well, eating any kind of debris.

# Gannets and Kittiwakes

These spectacular seabirds make their homes in coastal areas and on islands in different parts of the world. You can see the UK's largest mainland colonies of both gannets and kittiwakes on the Flamborough and Filey Coast.

## Courting Dance

Once male northern gannets choose nesting sites, they begin their courtship. This involves formally dipping, bowing, and spreading wings. Their elaborate performance will determine their mates, and pairs will often stay together for many years.

## CAPE KIDNAPPERS

Australasian gannets are found in New Zealand and Australian waters. They normally breed on offshore islands in large colonies, but one colony, also known as a gannetry, is located on the mainland at the oddly named Cape Kidnappers. In 1915, the area around the Cape Kidnappers gannetry was protected as a reserve.

# Take the Plunge

Gannets get their food by plunge-diving, tucking in their wings and shooting straight into the water at high speeds to catch their prey. The cape gannet, which lives off the coasts of Namibia and South Africa, can dive up to 60 miles per hour! Though most plunge dives are relatively shallow, northern gannets can go as deep as 72 feet.

Cape gannet

# Kittiwake Geography

Both red-legged and black-legged kittiwakes live in coastal areas of North America, but only the black-legged kittiwake can be found in Europe. "Kittiwake" is the name bestowed upon both species of gulls because of the loud, nasal "kitti-wake" call they make.

Juvenile gannets are generally dark brown or black. Over time, gannets gain increasing amounts of white feathers. They reach their adult plumage after four or five years.

Black-legged kittiwake

Red-legged kittiwake

Ahoy, mate! Kittiwakes tend to nest on cliff ledges, but they occasionally will use man-made structures such as buildings and even shipwrecks!

# In Danger

Endangered animals are species in danger of dying out due to both natural factors and human interference. Climate change, hunting, and pollution all contribute to the threat of extinction.

## Good Omens

Mediterranean monk seals were revered by the Greeks, and spotting a monk seal was said to be a good omen. One of the earliest known coins from around 500 B.C. depicted the head of a monk seal. The Mediterranean monk seal is one of the world's most endangered sea mammals, mainly threatened by human disturbance, including overfishing, pollution, and habitat loss from coastal development.

## Have a Heart

Hawksbill turtles are named for their birdlike beaks, and prized for their beautiful shells. Baby hawksbill shells are almost heart-shaped, elongating as the turtles become adults. Hawksbills are critically endangered due to shrinking coral reefs and nesting grounds, and because the turtles are often killed for their shells or accidentally caught in fishing nets.

# Icy Issue

Bearded seals are recognizable by their long, thick whiskers, which they use to find food underwater. These seals are one of the marine species at risk as the climate changes and ice continues to melt. These seals rely on the ice for their livelihood, spending time on it for feeding, resting, and birthing pups.

# Fishy Threats

Scalloped hammerhead sharks are not too particular about what they eat! They'll feed on bony fish, cephalopods, and some crustaceans, as well as sharks and rays. In some parts of the Pacific, they even eat sea snakes. In certain areas of the ocean, scalloped hammerheads gather in huge schools, sometimes up to hundreds of individuals, to migrate in the summer. These sharks are threatened by fishing, because their fins are desirable, and they are also a product of bycatch.

# Swimming Angels

Angel sharks spend much of their time hiding in the mud or sand, in relatively shallow waters. They are sometimes called monkfish or, interestingly enough, sand devils. Though angel sharks are protected by law in some countries, they remain vulnerable to bycatch, or accidental capture by large nets, in commercial fishing.

# Ray Days

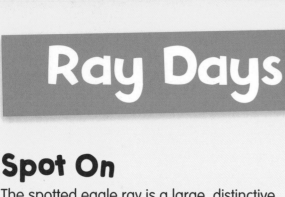

## Spot On

The spotted eagle ray is a large, distinctive animal. It can reach a width of 11 feet, making it one of the largest eagle rays. As its name suggests, this ray has white spots on the upper part of its blackish-blue body, and its underside is white. The snout is rounded and pointed at the tip, making it look like a bird's beak.

## Active Lifestyle

Spotted eagle rays are active swimmers and are always on the lookout for food. They are foraging predators and will eat a variety of invertebrates and small fish, like shrimp, crabs, octopuses, and bivalves.

Spotted eagle rays can give birth to litters of four pups at a time. The young live off the energy they obtain from yolk sacs inside the mothers. Once the pups can survive on their own, their mothers give birth.

# IT'S ELECTRIC!

Torpedo rays, also called electric rays, have the ability to produce electric shocks. They are found in warm and temperate waters and can range in size from 1 to 6 feet in length. The muscles that produce the shocks are located on either side of the ray's head and can emit shocks of up to 220 volts depending on the species—enough to injure a grown man.

The shocks of electric rays are used for defense, sensory location, and capturing prey. In ancient Greece and Rome, the shocks of the Atlantic ray served a different purpose: The Greeks and Romans used the shocks to treat headaches, gout, and other illnesses!

Electric rays are slow, sluggish animals that propel themselves with their tails instead of their pectoral fins and bodies like other rays. They lie in wait for their prey below the sand or from other hiding spots. When a fish gets too close, the ray will stun and capture it, eating it headfirst and whole.

# Boxy Fish

Cowfish and boxfish belong to the same fish family. They are easily picked out from the crowd because of their shapes, patterns, and colors.

## VARIETY SHOW

Despite their name, boxfish come in a variety of shapes, like triangles, squares, and pentagons, and an array of colors and patterns. When stressed, boxfish release a toxin that poisons nearby marine life. Because of this, boxfish don't make very good aquarium pets!

## Boxed In

The blue boxfish could be a turtle's cousin. It's covered with a tortoise-like shell except where its fins, eyes, and tail stick out. No bigger fish wants to take a bite out of this hardhead.

## Coat of Armor

Scrawled cowfish scales are stiff and fused together like plates of armor.

# Crack the Code

## Boxfish Family

Fill in the blanks to discover the names of two other members of the boxfish family. Look at each letter below, and write the letter that comes before it in the alphabet in the space above.

H _ _ _ _ _ _ _
  I  V  N  Q  C  B  D  L

T _ _ _ _ _ _ _ _ _
  U  V  S  S  F  U  G  J  T  I

H _ _ _ _ - _ _ _ _
  I  P  S  O   O  P  T  F

B _ _ _ _ _ _
  C  P  Y  G  J  T  I

# Rocking Out

## Rock On

Rock-boring urchins live in the Indo-Pacific region in tidepools, on exposed reef flats, and in rocks within a surge zone. They are the most common shallow-water urchins in Hawaii. The 2½-inch-wide urchins can be greenish-gray, tan, or pink, and have 100 to 150 spines. The rock-boring urchin gets its name from research that suggests the animal enlarges holes in the rock with its hard spines and scraping jaws so that it can hide from waves.The holes get bigger as the urchin grows. While inside its hole, the urchin eats any food caught inside, and it catches algae or seaweed with its spines, transferring the meal to its mouth using long, sucker-tipped tube feet.

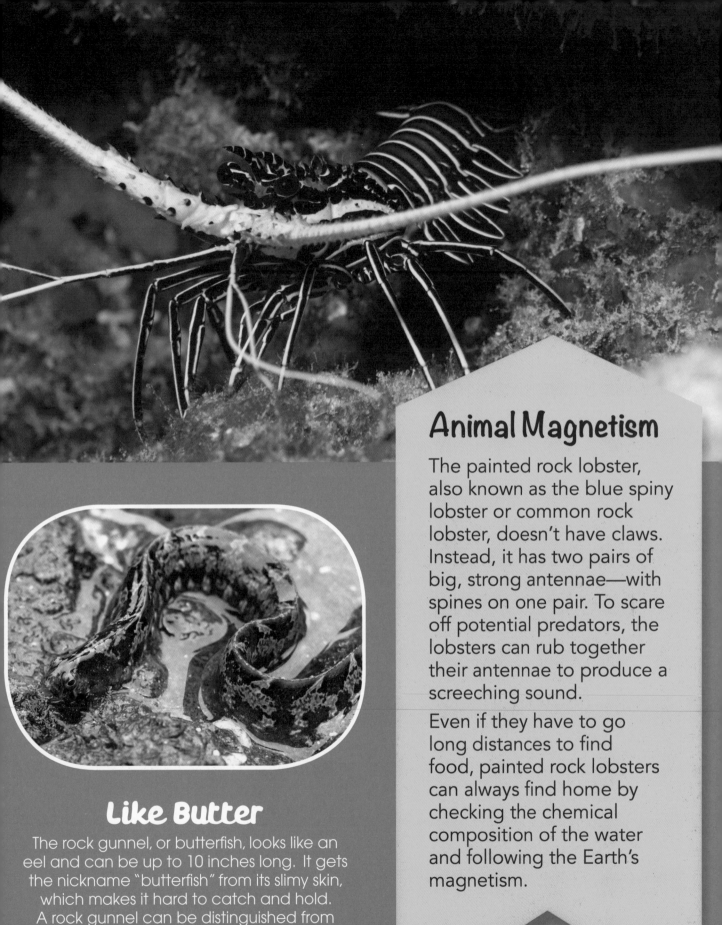

## Animal Magnetism

The painted rock lobster, also known as the blue spiny lobster or common rock lobster, doesn't have claws. Instead, it has two pairs of big, strong antennae—with spines on one pair. To scare off potential predators, the lobsters can rub together their antennae to produce a screeching sound.

Even if they have to go long distances to find food, painted rock lobsters can always find home by checking the chemical composition of the water and following the Earth's magnetism.

## Like Butter

The rock gunnel, or butterfish, looks like an eel and can be up to 10 inches long. It gets the nickname "butterfish" from its slimy skin, which makes it hard to catch and hold. A rock gunnel can be distinguished from similar-looking fish and eels by the distinctive black spots surrounded by a white ring that run along the base of the dorsal fin.

# Big Fish

## Body Slam

The giant trevally is a muscly predator with a strange hunting habit. It is a blitz-and-bump predator, meaning it rushes up to its prey and body slams it to stun or kill the victim. It then eats the fish, juvenile turtle, or small dolphin in one bite to prevent other giant trevally from stealing its food.

## False Lung

Tarpons are one of the few types of fish that have a swim bladder in addition to their gills. The swim bladder acts like a lung, allowing the fish to breathe raw air like humans do.

According to fossil record, tarpons have been around since prehistoric times. These fish can grow to 8 feet long and weigh up to 280 pounds. Because of their majestic size and color, they are often called silver kings.

Billfish, like blue marlins, have a blood vessel structure called a countercurrent exchanger that warms the eyes and brain to help the fish think faster and see more clearly, making them better hunters.

## ALL GROWN UP

The blue marlin is the largest Atlantic marlin and one of the biggest fish in the world! Female blue marlins can be nearly four times larger than males. Female blue marlins have reached lengths of 14 feet and can weigh more than 1,985 pounds. The average size of a blue marlin is 11 feet and 200 to 400 pounds. It's hard to believe that these fish start off life nearly microscopic!

## Going Tailing

White marlins are a smaller species of billfish. They only reach an average length of 9 feet and weigh approximately 180 pounds. The white marlin doesn't use its bill to slash or stun its prey. Instead, it overtakes it using speed. While swimming, white marlins will "tail," or swim close enough to the surface of the water that their dorsal fins will break the surface.

# Work with Sea Creatures

Have you ever wondered what it would be like to study sea animals for a living?

Would you like to work with sea creatures up close?

Take a look at these careers that are perfect for marine animal lovers.

## MARINE MAMMAL TRAINER

Marine mammal trainers care for aquatic mammals like sea lions, dolphins, whales, and seals, and teach them to perform certain behaviors. They provide animals with mental and physical exercise and make it easier for vets to give the mammals medical exams. Trainers also teach marine mammals to perform in shows.

## MARINE BIOLOGISTS

Marine biologists study living things in the ocean. Many marine biologists travel to collect and analyze data about sea creatures, plant life, and different environments, and often publish their research. Employers for marine biologists include zoos, aquariums, schools, laboratories, museums, conservation groups, or government agencies.

## AQUARISTS

Aquarists take care of marine animals in places such as aquariums, zoos, and research facilities, observing animal behavior, feeding animals, cleaning tanks, and monitoring water temperature and quality. Some aquarists design exhibits or give presentations to visitors.

## MARINE MAMMALOGISTS

Marine mammalogists are marine biologists that study sea mammals. They can focus on a group of mammals such as cetaceans or pinnipeds, or even a single species.

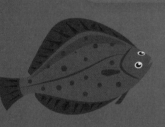

## AQUATIC VETERINARIANS

Aquatic veterinarians, or vets, are doctors just for marine animals! Aquatic vets often work in zoos, aquariums, museums, and marine parks.

## ICHTHYOLOGISTS

Ichthyologists are biologists that study fish, sharks, or rays.

# Help Save the Oceans

June 8 is World Oceans Day, but you don't have to limit your ocean-saving habits to one day a year. Here are a few ways you can help save the ocean every day, and some organizations that are already doing a great job.

| PROBLEM | SOLUTION |
|---|---|
| A big problem for the ocean is trash. Trash from the beaches and from everyday products that we throw out can end up in the ocean, causing massive problems for the ecosystem. Floating plastic often looks like food to birds, turtles, and mammals, but eating garbage will block an animal's digestive system and can cause it to choke or starve. | You can help reduce the amount of trash in the ocean in several ways: Use reusable bags and water bottles instead of plastic versions. When you go to the beach, make sure you pick up all your garbage and properly dispose of it. |
| When you are planting flowers or working in the yard, you may be hurting the ocean by using too much fertilizer. Excess fertilizer will eventually end up in the ocean which can result in a "dead zone," an area with very low oxygen levels. Since every living creature needs oxygen to survive, the fish are either killed or forced to leave the area. It can also cause algae blooms, which throws off the natural balance of the ocean. | One solution is to use less fertilizer in your garden and yard. Try composting if you really need the nutrients in your soil, since even manure can cause issues for the ocean. Another solution is to only grow plants that are natural to the area, since they won't need chemicals or fertilizers to help them grow. |
| Burning fossil fuels, like oil, gas, and coal, to power our homes adds carbon dioxide to the air and contributes to climate change. It also makes the ocean warmer and more acidic. Warming water hurts the fish that need cold water to live, as well as the Arctic animals we talked about in this book. When the ocean is more acidic, coral and clams have a harder time building their shells. | The easiest way to limit the amount of carbon dioxide released is to power down your life. Make sure you turn off lights and unplug chargers when not in use. Try using less air conditioning and taking shorter showers. Walk or ride your bike instead of taking a car. Little changes can make a big difference! If you can, talk to your parents about using clean sources of energy, like wind, solar, and/or geothermal. |

# ORGANIZATION

Take 3 is an Australian organization that encourages beachgoers to pick up three pieces of trash when they leave the beach. This helps clean up polluted beaches and prevents trash from entering the ocean. You can help by organizing a trash pickup day at your local beach with some friends!

The Surfrider Foundation is a grassroots organization that wants to preserve water quality and protect coastal ecosystems, beach access, and beach and surf spots. This organization is easy to join, and there are groups all over North America.

EarthEcho International is an organization dedicated to protecting all water sources and inspiring kids to work for a more sustainable future. Members monitor the water around the globe with help from the people that live there. EarthEcho International also has a Youth Leadership Council where teenagers develop programs that will help their countries be more sustainable.

# Legends of the Seas

Despite covering over 70% of the planet's surface and playing a major role in supporting life, only 5% of the ocean has been explored by humans. Much of the sea and marine life remains a mystery to us, leaving plenty of room for imagination.

## Bermuda Triangle

The fabled Bermuda Triangle, also called the Devil's Triangle, is an area of the Atlantic Ocean infamous for many mysterious shipwrecks and plane crashes. Legends tell of sea monsters, pirates, or even aliens attacking vessels or capturing humans, but the reality is far less outlandish: This part of the sea is heavily traveled, so more ships sink there than in areas with less traffic, and it's surrounded by a large coral reef that is difficult to sail over. Some of the deepest trenches in the ocean are in the Triangle, and most tropical storms in the Atlantic pass through it.

## ATLANTIS

The mythical city of Atlantis was said to be a perfect island civilization of half-god, half-human people whose lands were full of riches. When the people grew greedy, the gods sank the islands with fire and earthquakes. People have claimed that Atlantis was real, most commonly citing the volcanic destruction of the Greek island of Santorini about 3,600 years ago. In reality, the Greek philosopher Plato dreamed up this story centuries ago, likely to explain his moral philosophies.

# Fun Facts about Mythical Sea Creatures

## Kraken

The legend of the kraken came from Norway, where the gigantic sea monster was described as the size of a floating island and believed to attack ships and pull them into the depths of the sea. Sailors knew the kraken was coming when fish began rising to the ocean's surface. The kraken was likely based on the giant squid, which reportedly attacked ships a few times in the 1930s, or the colossal octopus.

## Mermaid

*Dugong*, the name of the animal that helped spark mermaid myths, means "lady of the sea" in the Malay language.

In 2012, a fake documentary called *Mermaids: The Body Found* aired on TV, convincing many people that mermaids were real!

## Hippocampus

The hippocampus was said to have the head and front legs of a horse and the lower part of a fish or dolphin. This "sea horse," found in Greek and Phoenician mythology, was said to draw the chariots of Poseidon and Neptune, the Greek and Roman gods of the sea.

## Sea Serpent

Sea serpents were often described as having dragon-like heads and spikes along their backs. These scary creatures may have been based on the elusive giant oarfish, which can grow up to 56 feet long. Some people think sailors were describing marine mammals such as the large elephant seal, shown at right.

# Answers

## Fill in the Blanks
### Secrets of the Sea

Fill in the missing letters to complete the fun ocean facts below. Then write the numbered letters in order at the bottom of the page to find out which sea creature is considered to be the largest animal that has ever lived!

The Pacific Ocean is the b i g g e s t ocean in the world.
1

The A t l a n t i c Ocean got its name from a Greek god.
2

Surrounding Antarctica, the S o u t h e r n Ocean is the
3    4
most recent addition to the named global oceans.

This whale species breaks through ice with its
skull: bo w h e a d.
5 6

Southern e l e p h a n t s e a l pups gain about 10 pounds
7         8
a day for a few weeks after birth.

Volcanoes and earthquakes around the edge of the
Pacific Ocean make up the R i n g o f F i r e.
9

Answer: The BLUE WHALE!

# Answers

## Spot the Difference

### Hidden Jewels

Find and circle 10 differences between these two pictures.

# Answers

# Word Search

## For the Birds

Look at the puzzle below and see if you can find the names of these seabirds. Circle the words going across, up and down, and diagonally. Some words may be backwards!

| | |
|---|---|
| AUK | KITTIWAKE |
| EIDER | PETREL |
| FULMAR | PUFFIN |
| GANNET | SEAGULL |
| HUMBOLDT PENGUIN | TERN |

```
J T P W N J W T V T S G L S Q
I W V L Q R H L N E J O Z P D
K G O L Z U R V C C Z N G F H
B N F U Y W B L Q Q M N Y M A
N I U G N E P T D L O B M U H
T U L A F Z K P A T K E C Q S
B E M E T O D A E P U F F I N
K U A S P X V N W Q E Y N D H
K F R B R Y N K Q I Y T U M P
S Y X Y Z A J I U Y T L R A Q
N M S E G E D E L A W T P E H
X L J T I I W A H R G U I H L
V U U D Y D Y Y S M F P W K C
O E E J A T E D Q I H I O J Z
N R E T Z Q D A A H C P G E F
```

300

## Page 57

# Maze

## Navigate the Nautilus

With its beautiful, creamy-colored shell and rust-colored stripes, the nautilus is highly sought after by shell collectors.

**Follow the maze from start to finish to get through the nautilus shell.**

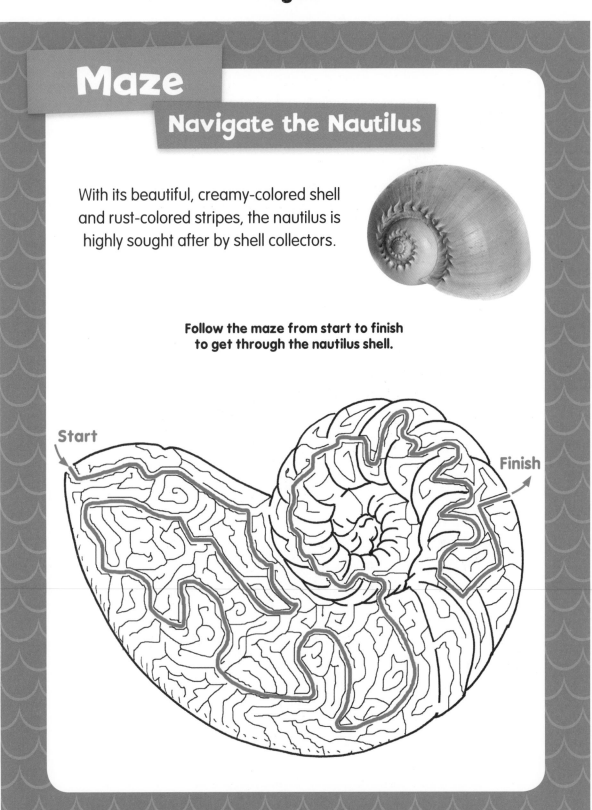

Start

Finish

## Page 71

# Pair Matching

## Conch Connections

Draw a line to connect each conch shell on the left with its match on the right.

# Answers

# Word Search

## Marine Animals

Look at the puzzle below and see if you can find the names of these marine animals. Circle the words going across, up and down, and diagonally. Some words may be backwards!

CALICO CRAB
CALICO BASS
HERMIT CRAB
BLOBFISH
GUITARFISH

SEA STAR
MANTA RAY
ATLANTIC SEA RAVEN
GUMMY SHARK
GREATER SOAPFISH

| A | T | L | A | N | T | I | C | S | E | A | R | A | V | E | N | O | P |
|---|---|---|---|---|---|---|---|---|---|---|---|---|---|---|---|---|---|
| D | B | D | F | Y | E | N | I | L | O | G | N | A | P | V | O | K | G |
| D | G | T | P | C | E | M | O | T | A | R | T | H | R | T | H | G | U |
| A | N | A | L | E | T | C | B | R | G | E | H | A | M | I | S | A | I |
| X | M | H | E | R | M | I | T | C | R | A | B | D | L | E | I | K | T |
| H | K | A | C | A | E | A | G | G | H | T | Y | R | O | K | F | L | A |
| C | W | D | N | E | B | A | Y | I | U | E | O | K | B | U | B | Y | R |
| A | C | B | R | T | P | E | D | I | B | R | I | O | T | A | O | R | F |
| L | Y | L | H | P | A | T | R | N | C | S | F | R | I | W | L | U | I |
| I | K | B | I | R | R | R | H | S | A | O | E | Q | S | R | B | M | S |
| C | S | F | N | V | A | G | A | A | B | A | L | A | O | T | A | M | H |
| O | O | N | O | B | O | M | R | Y | E | P | D | L | S | I | E | Y | P |
| C | D | Q | B | S | A | U | Z | K | Z | F | B | E | Y | T | F | S | H |
| R | K | I | I | F | F | S | S | O | B | I | J | F | R | G | A | H | S |
| A | Q | C | A | L | I | C | O | B | A | S | S | B | V | U | C | R | A |
| B | M | A | B | G | U | M | M | Y | S | H | A | R | K | T | R | A | Q |

# Answers

## Word Scramble

### Not Your Average Fish

Unscramble the letters to find the names of some amazing echinoderms and mollusks.

| | |
|---|---|
| ESA CURNHI | SEA URCHIN |
| ADSN DLRALO | SAND DOLLAR |
| ASE IYLL | SEA LILY |
| RATFEHE ARTS | FEATHER STAR |
| AES CMUCRUBE | SEA CUCUMBER |
| SOYRET | OYSTER |
| SELSUM | MUSSEL |
| LSACLPO | SCALLOP |
| MLAC | CLAM |
| NHCNO | CONCH |

## Page 121

## Crack the Code
### Dolphinfish

The common dolphinfish is not related to dolphins at all. It is a large, colorful tropical fish that plays an important role in the ocean food chain. Dolphinfish eat squids, open ocean crustaceans, and small fish, and they are food for sharks and other large predators. These fish are iridescent and beautifully colored, often blue, green, and gold with black spots.

Fill in the blanks to find out the common dolphinfish's Hawaiian name and the name of its closest relative. Look at each letter below, and write the letter that comes before it in the alphabet in the space above.

M A H I - M A H I
N B I J   N B I J

P O M P A N O   **DOLPHINFISH**
Q P N Q B O P

# Answers

## Search & Find®
### Peacock Flounder Peek-a-Boo

Search & Find® these 5 different peacock flounders among
the coral, seaweed, and other animals below.

## Page 147

# Word Search

## A Whale of a Word Search

Look at the puzzle below and see if you can find these words and names of animals in the whale family. Circle the words going across, up and down, and diagonally. Some words may be backwards!

| | |
|---|---|
| BALEEN | HARBOR PORPOISE |
| ORCA | HUMPBACK WHALE |
| SPERM WHALE | BOTTLENOSE DOLPHIN |
| CETACEAN | ODONTOCETI |
| BELUGA WHALE | NARWHAL |

```
B X H A R B O R P O R P O I S E D
D O D B Y E N I L O G N A P O R P
D C T B V B K O H H S T H R N E A
A E Z L E S E O D O N T O C E T I
X L G A L P G L Y W Q N D L S W K
H A W C H E A G U R N Y R L P S O
G H D K E R N Y I G Q A K I O R R
D W B R Y M S O T B A K R R U C K
A K L H P W T A S K B W J W Y E E
A C B I R H N H R E A O H G H T A
J A R N V A G A A K D L N A C A I
B B N O B L M R P N F O R R L C L
Y P Q B I E U Z E Z V A L Y Q E H
I M I T F F S E O B B J R P Q A K
R U E Y G X L K Y T B L B V H A A
A H C N E A C L O L T A O M P I B
O W A R B L E D W H E L A B T T N
```

# Answers

## Pair Matching

### Crocodile Conundrum

There are 5 crocodiles in each box, but only 3 matching pairs. Draw a line to connect 3 crocodiles in the top box to their identical twins in the box below.

# Answers

## Word Scramble
### Under the Sea

Unscramble the letters to find the names of some fascinating water-dwelling animals.

**HILNIFSO**
L I O N F I S H

**ROUGPER**
G R O U P E R

**LEBU EWLAH**
B L U E  W H A L E

**KHELW**
W H E L K

**TABTE ISFH**
B E T T A  F I S H

**GRERHNI**
H E R R I N G

**TRAGE EHWIT KAHSR**
G R E A T  W H I T E  S H A R K

**NOMO FELISLYJH**
M O O N  J E L L Y F I S H

**NIGAT DUSIQ**
G I A N T  S Q U I D

**ACDNIRAL HSFI**
C A R D I N A L  F I S H

# Answers

## Crack the Code

### Secrets of the Sea

Use the key below to crack the code and find out which sea creatures produce venom that is being studied or used to create medication for humans.

A=1  C=2  E=3  I=4  L=5  M=6  N=7  O=8  S=9

S E A     A N E M O N E
9 3 1     1 7 3 6 8 7 3

C O N E     S N A I L
2 8 7 3     9 7 1 4 5

## Page 223

# Pair Matching

## Poisonous Partners

There are 3 types of ocean residents below:
sea nettles, men o' war, and stingrays.
Draw a line to connect each of the 3 pairs
of identical twins.

# Answers

## Page 235

**Maze**

**Rockin' Rays**

These 2 rays are hunting for a meal. Help the manta ray get to the plankton and the stingray find a fish in the sand.

Start

Start

Stingray

Manta ray

Fish

Finish

Finish

## Page 249

# Word Scramble

## Watery Words

Unscramble the letters to find the names of some interesting sea animals.

LOCICA  BACR
C A L I C O   C R A B

INF  HAELW
F I N   W H A L E

AZDLRI  IFHS
L I Z A R D   F I S H

TANIG  FIHORFGS
G I A N T   F R O G F I S H

TEMHMOGUA  KHASR
M E G A M O U T H   S H A R K

KASHIBLWL  RUTTEL
H A W K S B I L L   T U R T L E

ONOCTUC  TOPOCSU
C O C O N U T   O C T O P U S

GYPYM  ESA  SHEOR
P Y G M Y   S E A   H O R S E

DOSIREL  BACR
S O L D I E R   C R A B

# Answers

## Spot the Difference
### Sea Pen Pandemonium

Find and circle 5 differences between these two pictures of sea pens.

# Answers

# Underwater Maze

## Cats of the Sea

Help the leopard shark get back to the seafloor. Make sure to avoid the tiger shark, which might just make the leopard shark its dinner!

# Answers

## Crack the Code
### Boxfish Family

Fill in the blanks to discover the names of two other members of the boxfish family. Look at each letter below, and write the letter that comes before it in the alphabet in the space above.

H U M P B A C K
I V N Q C B D L

T U R R E T F I S H
U V S S F U G J T I

H O R N - N O S E
I P S O   O P T F

B O X F I S H
C P Y G J T I